Transform your Training

Develop and deliver training that
changes lives in the criminal justice,
social care and charity sectors

Tammy Banks

Rethink

First published in Great Britain in 2020
by Rethink Press (www.rethinkpress.com)

© Copyright Tammy Banks

Contents

Introduction

I was a child born into a cycle of harm, abuse and chaos. Professionals helped me to change my life and, as a result, I'm now fulfilled, contributing to society and making a positive impact. My children will never experience the devastation I did. They already believe the world is full of possibilities and that they are loved beyond measure. Cycle ended.

I've been on the receiving end of support from frontline workers, and I have been the frontline professional too, starting as a support worker and moving through the ranks to CEO. Since graduating, I have spent nearly twenty years working in charities, criminal justice and social care.

Back in 2016, my friend Faye Fox and I were working as operational and strategic managers within criminal justice, a sector we had worked in for several years. We developed our company, Taye Training, to meet our service delivery needs, which in our experience weren't being met by other training on offer. Taye Training started with Faye and me delivering the sessions personally, but demand soon grew, so we built a national team of operational experts to deliver courses to organisations that have connected experience.

We received phenomenal feedback. Curious, we analysed thousands of sessions to find out why delegates enjoyed our training so much. The results have shown they value the fact that the facilitators are operational experts and can connect the learning to the delegates' organisation and job role. They found all our materials to be high-quality and based on best practice and legislation, and love that we presented the information with consideration to different learning styles.

What has made a big difference to the feedback is that Taye's team all consistently deliver from the same values-based perspective. These values, which are so intrinsic to our services, are consciously interwoven throughout all sessions. We value the frontline professional and their end customer equally. We recognise that each professional has their own home life and needs to have their emotional resilience topped up regularly, to enable them to continue positively delivering services. When we consistently deliver from this perspective we help our frontline professionals to avoid burnout and stay motivated, enabling them to deliver services which prioritise their customer and to make decisions on their behalf (where needed) that are values-based in their execution.

This is why 'values-led' became the golden thread of our methodology, a methodology we have chosen to name 'Training 4 Influence'. This methodology was born out of the feedback we received and forms the core of this book.

Recently, after one of our training sessions, a delegate talked about our approach. She referred to it as delivering 'subliminal' messages. I laughed out loud, but she has a point. Every training session the Taye Training team delivers is about encouraging and influencing the culture in statutory criminal justice, social care and charities, and recognising the importance of people. Staff members are not a commodity and a client is not a number. We are all people; there is no 'us and them', just 'us and we'.

Through recognising and helping to develop the Training 4 Influence methodology, I have an opportunity to influence many more lives. The more Taye's team and I connect groups, break down barriers and value people, the more we will absolutely disrupt the generational cycle of harm, abuse and chaos. This will impact society. This will mean change.

Taye Training now delivers nationally. We have contracts with area authorities, police, prisons and charities, both large and local. We deliver mandatory and specialist training, and we deliver it adhering to the Training 4 Influence methodology.

I hope this book either reinforces the things you already know or transforms your training. Either way, if you follow the principles, your training will have added influence and be the best it can possibly be.

I hope you enjoy reading this book as much as I've enjoyed writing it.

1
How The Training 4 Influence Methodology Was Developed

Taye Training developed the Training 4 Influence methodology in response to growing pressure within the criminal justice, social care and charity sectors with people being asked to deliver more for less. It has been designed specifically to add value and influence on the frontline, despite policy change and austerity measures, and to have immediate operational impact in the areas that I've always worked in, that I love. But it can be used in other sectors too. The examples throughout this book are specific to my experience, but the methodology is transferrable.

Training 4 Influence is a creative solution, a methodology that can transform any training session, weaving golden threads that improve organisational outcomes without costing the delegate or commissioner any more time or money than they are spending now. The method ensures training is delivered in a way that inspires, is relevant, enables learning and meets objectives. This ensures that frontline workers are skilled, knowledgeable and qualified, and that they leave sessions enthusing about how their activities in their day job are going to be improved as a result of the training.

When the method is followed in its entirety, the magic happens. Training using this method ensures that frontline professionals feel valued, have a person-centred approach and benefit from the emotional resilience and motivation to deliver exceptional services to some of the most complex, marginalised and vulnerable in our society. The principles also focus on rebuilding and reconnecting the delegate to their own mission and the mission of the organisation they are working for. They recognise that people are an organisation's biggest asset, and if we want them to deliver services that change lives; we need to ensure they know they matter. It isn't just about doing a job; it's a vocation, an opportunity and a privilege to work in a frontline role.

We could have developed a training course that simply focused on taking a values-based approach and building emotional resilience, but we didn't. There are loads of courses, short and long, that already do this, and do it well. The stark truth is that most frontline professionals don't have the time or brain space for extra study or personal development, so they need something different.

Some training is mandated and regulated. Quality assurers, commissioners and sector leaders insist on it. Training 4 Influence transforms any training session. If an organisation can only manage to provide mandatory sessions for their staff, the Training 4 Influence method will still have influence.

This book has been written for trainers and facilitators. You may work within an organisation and train internally, or you may train as a consultant or have your own company. You may even be reading this as part of your induction to delivering training with Taye. Either way, the only prerequisite is that you currently or intend to deliver training.

Predominantly, I expect the people reading this book to be delivering training to professionals working with children and adults who have complex needs, are vulnerable and/or experiencing multiple disadvantages. This doesn't mean that the principles are not relevant to other sectors; it just means that this book wasn't written with them in mind.

As you've picked up this particular book, I guess you recognise the power that training can have and how, collectively, we can make a real difference in the sector. I am also guessing you have found there's something missing from the training qualifications on the market today – the ones which teach delivery techniques to anyone who enrols, regardless of their business sector.

This book will show you how to use the Training 4 Influence four-step methodology to:

- Transform your training

- Influence organisational outcomes

- Change lives

Imagine if we eliminated boring, unconnected, unin-spiring training sessions. Imagine if everyone who ever delivered training to frontline professionals – the people perfectly positioned to change lives – used the Training 4 Influence method. What a difference we could make collectively.

The Training 4 Influence method influences people's values and approach, helping them recognise their biases and build their emotional resilience, all while delivering expert, engaging and inspirational train-ing. This training absolutely supports the individuals working in the sector to feel valued, enabling them to continue transforming lives.

This book has been written to introduce you to each element of Training 4 Influence. Before we start, allow me to take you step by step through the methodology, explaining why each step is of equal importance. Con-necting them all together is when the magic happens.

What is Training 4 Influence?

The four-step method is:

1. Expert – Training that is delivered by an expert.

   - Facilitators with connected operational experience can share examples, bring alive the learning, motivate and inspire.

   - Facilitators with excellent delivery and communication skills are adept at listening, questioning, explaining concepts and giving feedback.

2. Tailored – Training that is tailored to the sector, organisation and customer group.

   - The subject matter is clear, adheres to legislation and is written to exceed industry quality standards.

   - Facilitators who have an understanding of the organisation, team and individuals enable sessions to connect to objectives, mission, policies, processes and case examples and can explore any complex staff dynamics.

3. Engaging – We all learn differently, and it is important that each delegate has their personal learning needs met. The methodology explores

   - Accelerated learning techniques.

   - Different learning styles.

- The importance of variety.

- Multiple intelligences.

4. Values – The golden thread that connects together the method is delivering from a values-based perspective and enabling change to happen, including:

    - Your values as a facilitator.

    - Values-based decision making.

    - How you value others.

    - How you value yourself.

The methodology focuses specifically on how to ensure each element is achieved – on how to have influence. On its own, each step makes a difference, but, collectively, they are game changers. This book will take you through the elements of the method, explaining the difference that each makes, and why, when they are all combined, the magic happens. If you're a trainer, you can use the principles and learning from this book to increase the influence your training has, or decide to become a fully accredited Training 4 Influence facilitator.

Collectively we believe this can make a huge difference to how services are delivered to some of the most complex customers. This blueprint has been developed and refined in the criminal justice, social care, statutory and charity sectors, as this is where my experience lies and where I identified a need for tailored training to help people working with complex needs. But the principles hold good for other types of training too. In fact, it's my belief that this is the only way to deliver training that properly meets the needs of any organisation or company.

There are so many different reasons why I decided to write this book. When I look at them as a whole, though, I realise that every single one is directly or indirectly about recognising that we all have the power to change someone's life. And I truly believe everything that has happened to me has led me to this point.

That may sound a little over the top. After all, this is a book about a training methodology, not about changing the world. But the methodology was developed to change the world. Even if it changes things for one person at a time, it's about changing *their* world. Collectively, we can use the Training 4 Influence methodology to make much better use of our precious limited resources.

For you, the trainer, having a method to follow is both liberating and affirming. It enables you to help transform the frontline professional sitting in front of you, so that they are no longer frustrated and disconnected from their mission, and feel re-motivated and equipped with the skills and confidence to do their job to the best of their ability. And ultimately, it helps to transform the lives of the complex and/or vulnerable people who access your trainees' services and find they are expert, inclusive and transformational.

My past

Let me explain the personal relevance of Training 4 Influence in a little more detail. I was a child heading nowhere fast when a frontline professional started the domino effect that absolutely changed my life. She helped me navigate a broken system and gave me permission to value myself. Without her, I have no idea where I would be today, and so I truly understand the difference one person can make to someone's life.

The life I'd had before her intervention was troubled. I grew up in a less than ideal home situation, leaving school without any GCSEs and finding myself homeless at the age of fifteen. It was a chaotic and dangerous time. My days were full of adversity and making the wrong choices. I wouldn't repeat those days, but equally, I wouldn't delete them. The lessons I learned, the actions I took to survive and the people I lost, I will never forget. They gave me the values and principles I live by today. They also enabled me to see past someone's physical appearance, behaviour and living situation to access what is important and who they really are.

I will never forget the feelings of hopelessness, being overwhelmed and powerlessness. These emotions are what nearly destroyed me, but they're also what propelled me forward, one step at a time. I was lucky because, through sheer stubbornness and the help of one visionary teacher, I was able to attend college while living homeless, and eventually managed to gain a place to study psychology at university.

Going from living in a hostel where most of us were disconnected from our families, desperate and in survival mode, to moving into the university halls of residence was a *Sliding Doors* moment for me. Although the journey nearly crushed me, the learning was immense. I realised that in the right environment, with the right human connection and the right opportunities, anyone can achieve anything.

And because that one frontline worker demonstrated she understood and valued me as an individual, the cycle of abuse and harm stopped with me, and my children are free to experience a positive environment and grow up into fulfilled adults. I am forever thankful to her.

My personal experience has led me to understand that I want to increase opportunities for people who are vulnerable, marginalised and have complex needs, helping them reach their potential and be happy, whatever that may mean to them. To truly interrupt the generational cycle of abuse, harm and poverty, we need to work positively with people who are at risk of causing harm. If we can prevent that harm happening, we prevent someone becoming a victim. If we prevent them becoming a victim, we prevent the impact of trauma and the potential myriad consequences, including substance misuse, homelessness, offending and mental-health problems.

I have literally been the person frontline professionals are seeking to safeguard or support to transform their lives. I was living a chaotic and complex life and I was far more connected to the homeless community than I was to the idea of opportunity. I didn't believe I had positive choices open to me.

One person stepped in and gave me the power to transform my life and, over the years, I have come to reflect on what her back-story might have been. What pressures was she under when she was working with me? How much training and support was she given? Could she have changed even more lives if she had attended regular training delivered by a facilitator who used the Training 4 Influence method?

I've been on the receiving end of support from frontline workers, and I have been the frontline professional, too, starting as support worker and moving through the ranks to CEO. Since graduating, I have spent nearly twenty years working in charities, criminal justice and social-care services.

If you think it's no coincidence that I ended up working in this sector, you're absolutely correct. Once I got my life on track, I realised it was heading in one direction – to work with people who are like I once was. I wanted to be the person to help them change their lives.

I've heard it said that the two most important days in your life are the day you are born and the day you find your why. I've found my why. I have always worked with people experiencing multiple disadvantages and/or increased vulnerabilities. People who either are victims of harm or have harmed others. More often than not, they are both.

As a frontline worker, I always sought out the most complex situation and tried to change it. Initially, I worked operationally with individuals in children's homes, prisons and homeless hostels. I was the support worker balancing the importance of building relationships with professional boundaries and meeting my targets, getting my paperwork finished among emergency situations and increasing caseloads.

Over the years, I moved into more strategic roles. On behalf of the local authority, I managed homeless hostels and housing and traveller sites before moving into the charity sector. I designed and led young people's homeless services, becoming a regional safeguarding manager. And then, for six years, I worked as a CEO of a charity operating on behalf of the probation service and the police to rehabilitate high risk people convicted of offences who were living in the community.

Naively, as my career progressed, I thought management and leadership would be easy. Of course, it isn't. Strategic positions are still full of people who care, and I was still under pressure and working passionately to make change.

A sector in crisis

I'm lucky that I've always loved my work, but the social care, criminal justice and charity sectors are in crisis. Funding is being withdrawn, caseloads are growing, services are closing. Competitive tenders mean collaboration is disappearing, passionate staff are burning out and leaving for the sake of their own mental health, and those who stay are trying to deliver a quality service to customers amid organisational and political chaos.

I have grown tired of watching good staff struggle. To be completely honest, I became frustrated. The most vulnerable people in our society often don't receive the support they need because of the struggles the frontline professionals are facing. Due to external factors, these professionals cannot have an impact, further highlighting powerlessness. Every person deserves to live a fulfilled life, professionals and service users alike. I want to be the someone who can help change the lives of frontline workers and their colleagues.

As a manager, I searched for organisations that could help by delivering training to my team to upskill, empower and motivate them, but I found only generic courses that didn't relate properly to my sector. These courses only skimmed the surface of what I was looking for, or were too general to be useful to those working with complex needs. Everything I found seemed to offer so much, but in reality delivered little. It was effectively a tick-box exercise and staff were feeding back that their training day would have been better spent supporting customers, changing lives and reducing their workload. This frustrated me even more, as staff time and motivation are precious resources.

How can you positively impact someone else's life if every day is a struggle for you? I realised that I desperately wanted to help on a bigger scale, which puts me in mind of an old parable.

THE BOY AND THE STARFISH[1]

One day, an old man was walking along a beach littered with thousands of starfish that had been washed ashore by the high tide. As he walked, he came upon a young

---

1   L Eiseley, *The Star Thrower* (Harcourt Ltd, 1979)

boy who was eagerly throwing the starfish back into the ocean, one by one.

Puzzled, the man looked at the boy and asked what he was doing. Without looking up from his task, the boy replied simply.

'I'm saving these starfish, sir.'

The old man chuckled. 'Son, there are thousands of starfish and only one of you. What difference can you make?'

The boy picked up a starfish, gently tossed it into the water and turned to the man.

'I made a difference to that one,' he said.

If one person can change one other person's life, what can be achieved by many?

When I was working as a regional safeguarding manager, I discovered the power of talking to a roomful of professionals. I discovered the difference that I could make by taking the time to support the people who are expected to support others. I learned that I had a talent for developing bespoke training solutions and delivering these solutions one-to-one, or for up to 400 people at a time, making exactly the impact that I was looking for.

When I made the decision to set up Taye Training with my colleague and friend, Faye Fox, we knew that we wanted to deliver, to those working with people who have complex needs, a quality in-depth training tailored to their role, team, organisation and specific requirements. More than that, we wanted to share our values-based approach and what we had learned about really appreciating professionals to enable them to continue transforming lives.

I've worked in the sector for long enough to recognise the importance of added value. We are literally seeking creative solutions. Times are tough, there is not enough money to undertake all the tasks our customers need and our commissioners expect, yet we are still passionate about and dedicated to making change, achieving our mission and positively impacting society.

Taye Training's journey has been about helping people who do vitally important work to gain the skills and resilience they need to deliver essential services to those with complex needs, and helping organisations to maximise the return on their investment in training. There is a clear methodology to our sessions and, in this book, I'm going to share it with you. I'm excited about the impact we can all ultimately have on people who need frontline services. The Training 4 Influence methodology is my creative response to an over-stretched and under-resourced criminal justice and social care system. It delivers learning objectives while motivating and empowering frontline professionals to have a person-centred, values-based approach.

The purpose of this book is to take you through the methodology in a logical and detailed way, explaining why we do what we do so that you understand the importance of each step and how it fits into the overall plan. Each of the next four chapters will focus on one element of the Training 4 Influence methodology, providing information, advice, processes, techniques and case examples. There may be a textbook feel to it in places as I explain the theory, but my aim is to bring to life the concept and detail of Training 4 Influence in an accessible and useable way. If, as you are reading, you are curious to assess how much of the techniques I explain you already use and how much added influence your training offers, visit the Training 4 Influence website and take the quick self-assessment questionnaire at https://training4influence.co.uk/resources/. It takes just ten minutes and you will receive feedback based on your current delivery style.

2
Expert

In this chapter, we are going to focus on the first step of the Training 4 Influence methodology. This step is the one that makes the other three elements possible.

Whatever our feelings are about training courses, we've probably all been in a position where we've attended one and found that it didn't meet our needs. The trainer didn't understand the pressures we're under, the course wasn't specific to our sector (or the particular people that we provide a service to), and we were left with unanswered questions and a feeling of frustration at the wasted day, and at the growing pile of work that would be waiting for us when we got back to the office. Alternatively, if you're a trainer, you may have previously dusted off a one-size-fits-all course and delivered it the way you've always delivered it, because that's what you were asked to do.

Does any of this sound familiar?

Now, picture a different scene. You arrive at the course. The facilitator has lots of experience in the type of complex needs you work with and is an expert in the subject area. They know the context in which you're operating, they understand the pressure you're under and they've designed the course for you. All the examples and activities are relevant to your role, and the facilitator has even included a session on helping you to build your emotional resilience. You leave feeling re-energised and you've learned something that will really benefit you in the days, months and years to come.

When Faye and I first set up Taye Training, that was the vision we had. We wanted people working in a sector that is stretched almost to breaking point to receive high-quality training that would make a difference to their lives, and to the lives of their customers. And it would have to be affordable, too.

When an operational expert is delivering a session, they bring more than just experiences and examples to bear. They also bring a true understanding of the sector, the customer group and how to facilitate the learning objectives in a way that will influence a delegate's daily work. An operational expert can reassure, advise and guide delegates through the learning process. They can explore the implications of legislation or restrictions based on commissioned targets – training facilitated by someone who has walked the walk is inspirational. That's why having an operational expert delivering the training is a fundamental and essential part of Taye's methodology.

CASE EXAMPLE

At a Taye recruitment event, one of the attendees (a recently retired police officer) said he'd worked in his station's training department for years. The approach was that any qualified trainer could deliver any material. No sooner had he finished talking than another attendee said she worked for a national charity and its approach was the same.

Having facilitators who are operational experts is one of the cornerstones of Taye Training. We wouldn't deliver training any other way.

What an operational expert requires

Please don't feel overwhelmed by the expression 'operational expert' or think that this can't possibly be you. I am not referring to needing an encyclopaedic knowledge of a subject or a string of academic qualifications after your name. For the purposes of the Training 4 Influence methodology, an operational expert within a certain sector means someone who has experience of one or more of:

- Undertaking a similar role to the delegates – voluntarily or paid
- Working in a connected field
- Working with the customer group
- Real-life with the customer group
- Personal connections with the customer group

This will normally mean people who have current experience, but it could also be historic experience if you've been keeping up to date with key changes and are willing to undertake further studies or co-facilitate with someone with more experience. You can also be an operational expert if your experience is personal, although you may wish to think about the timing and potential impact on your life. In addition, you will normally be delivering or want to deliver in sectors you already know.

Hopefully, as you're reading this chapter, you're nodding your head and thinking that I'm not telling you anything you don't already know. But even if you feel you are not an operational expert in the area in which you currently deliver training, all is not lost.

If you work internally in a training department for a large organisation, you may have been recruited to the role without needing any specialism. At Taye, we regularly work in partnership with learning and development teams and organisational trainers for exactly this reason.

CASE EXAMPLE

I first realised the power of being an operational expert when I was delivering training as part of my role for a national charity. I'd been matched with an organisation to help its people become safeguarding excellent. This included training, coaching and conferences. I loved bringing safeguarding alive using my experiences from working with prisons, children's homes and homelessness, and watching the penny drop. Safeguarding is important; it literally saves lives.

When that project ended, many organisations asked me to continue delivering training. I was astounded at the difference my experience was making.

When Faye and I started Taye, we had a skeleton presentation that was followed for a course, but most of the content that we delivered was based around context, examples and encouraging people to share their thoughts. We were naturally supportive throughout, as we recognise that working with people who have complex needs and vulnerabilities and are experiencing multiple disadvantages is hard enough. And since then, it has become our passion to support people to reach their full potential. Delegates need to know that we all struggle at times, but that's OK as long as we have the support, processes and values in place.

It may sound like the importance of being an operational expert was always obvious to us, but it wasn't, because neither Faye nor I saw ourselves as one, just as you may not see yourself as one. That doesn't mean you aren't.

For personal reasons, Faye and I have always chosen to work in the criminal justice, social care and charity sectors, and have gathered years' worth of experience and examples along the way. If you work in the same sectors, you may recognise some of these issues:

- Increasingly high caseloads and a lack of experienced staff to deal with them

- Short-term agency staff or inexperienced staff being recruited and struggling to find their way in their roles

- Short-term contracts leading to insecurity and high turnover

- Staff being under phenomenal pressure, demotivated and in danger of feeling overwhelmed and burning out

There is a danger of lowering standards and inconsistency of practice. Customers' concerns are being missed. Budgets are stretched, services are being recommissioned, and funding is being withdrawn in some cases. Organisations are not delivering in line with their mission and values, and the customers at the end of all of this continue to live in crisis. This is when their risk of harm or even death increases.

An operational expert understands those struggles. By following the Training 4 Influence method, they can help to make staff more effective in their roles and more resilient to enhance their wellbeing. They can work with teams to improve dynamics. They can help with maintaining standards and consistency, weaving the mission, values, policies and processes through everything an organisation does so that these are rein-forced and brought to life. Through their work with the staff, they can improve things for customers. Ulti-mately, they help organisations to get the most from their training budgets.

The power of experience

At Taye, we don't expect our facilitators to be qualified / experienced trainers when they apply to us. It's great if they are, but it's not a prerequisite. What we do want them to have is current operational experience with vulnerable people or people with complex needs. We want them to have similar values and prin-ciples to our own, in relation to the work that they do. The golden thread that runs through everything Taye Training does is that we make it person-centred and value everybody.

I also understand the need to make training budgets stretch further. I know only too well the true costs of ineffective training, or training that doesn't hit the mark. It's not just the financial cost of the course itself; it's the cost of having people out of the office for a day or longer, when their time could be better spent elsewhere. Resources are too precious to spend on something that holds little or no value.

I would strongly recommend that all course facilitators only train delegates on courses they have operational experience in themselves. Let me share a case example that highlights how much I value operational expertise. This example shows how being an operational expert helped me to help another professional in a training session.

CASE EXAMPLE

A delegate attending one of Taye's courses was unhappy about the fact that her concerns were being dismissed by the local authority. She was a housing support worker and had raised a safeguarding concern about a young person she had been working with for six months. She had amassed much evidence of this person's change in behaviour, but felt she was viewed as 'just' a housing support worker who wasn't qualified, despite having ten years' experience working with complex young people.

In the session, with her permission, we used her example as an activity. We broke down her referral and the subsequent complex conversations with the local authority. In the group discussions that followed, I gave examples of times I have rewritten referrals over and over again, and of heated discussions I've had on child-protection panels.

We talked through how social workers are busy professionals who can't just 'take your word for it'; they need evidence presented in an understandable way. They haven't seen the changes in the young person for themselves and will be assessing against local thresholds.

My brief assessment of the young person was that she did indeed meet the local threshold for a statutory assessment. We then, as extra reassurance, talked through the escalation process.

Interestingly, the housing support worker phoned me a fortnight later and explained that she had sent her rewritten referral to and arranged a call with the assessment team. She had also, after her conversation with me in the training, dismissed her thoughts of being judged as lesser than a qualified social worker, which had been a barrier for her. The new referral had been accepted. All she had needed were the skills to write a referral while understanding thresholds and having the belief in her professional judgement. Because I have walked this path many times, I could give her examples and reassure her effectively.

The example demonstrates the added benefit of an operational expert delivering the course. I had gone to the session to deliver clearly defined safeguarding training, but in addition to this, I was able to give a delegate the opportunity to debrief, vent, explore different approaches with others, feel heard, build understanding and practise a new technique. She then applied that technique in her daily role and had a safeguarding referral accepted as a result. This may seem like a small victory, but every decision in safeguarding can make a significant impact and prevent harm. The delegate felt encouraged and capable. She witnessed the change in response, based on her change in approach. Powerful stuff.

Here's the thing: being an operational expert isn't about having all the knowledge; it's about true experience, understating and empathy. Facilitators need to be inspirational and engaging. They need to speak the delegates' language and demonstrate their belief in the subject they are facilitating.

There are so many benefits to having an operational expert delivering the training course, but there is one big elephant in the room...

Are you the right facilitator?

This has been a struggle for me personally. In the early Taye days, Faye and I were surprised that people kept asking us to deliver training for them, and the company grew from there. Because of this, way before Training 4 Influence was ever considered, we'd locked down 'being an operational expert' as Taye's unique selling point and built our business by recruiting others with frontline experience.

A few years on, Faye and I can be matched with subjects such as leadership and governance but, more often than not, when an organisation contacts us now to develop or deliver training for their teams on the frontline, we utilise the expertise of a facilitator who has more current or connected experience than us.

We have facilitators who work with the police, charities, housing, probation, homelessness, social care and schools. I'm confident that all our trainers are excellent at what they do, especially as they are all trained in at least one of Taye's core suite of courses:

- Safeguarding
- Equality and diversity
- Managing challenging behaviour
- Principles of risk management
- Professional boundaries
- Lone working

You'll no doubt have noticed I use the term 'facilitator' rather than 'trainer'. This is another nod to the importance of the facilitator having connected experience and understanding the delegates' sector or customer group. I believe the best trainers facilitate learning, rather than teaching. Yes, there is always some new information to share and learn from, but how that is done is really important. Conversations and shared practice need to be encouraged.

In the sectors Taye deals with, many quality assurers make it mandatory for frontline workers to attend training sessions every three years. That means that we could have extremely experienced and knowledgeable workers in the session alongside brand-new people on their induction. With our knowledge and experience of the sector, we can facilitate the session effectively so everyone's learning needs are met, encouraging the more experienced delegates to share the knowledge they have amassed over the years.

If you are a freelance facilitator, I would urge you to use the method I've just described yourself when you are asked to deliver a session. Consider whether you are the best person for the job. Do you have the connected operational experience? It's a slippery slope to possible reputational damage if you take jobs that do not match your expertise. The pound signs can be tempting, but the impact you have may not be so beneficial and the feedback you receive at the end of the session may not be kind.

If you work within an organisation as a trainer, this may be more difficult for you. There may be certain courses that you are expected to deliver. Where possible, I'd recommend having honest conversations with your manager. If no one else can deliver the sessions, maybe an operational worker can co-facilitate with you. You can cover the objectives of the course and they can contextualise it. Or alternatively, you may be able to partner with an outside organisation, like Taye, that can either run the session for you (while you focus on developing your expertise) or work with you as the operational expert.

What makes a great facilitator?

As we've already seen, being an operational expert doesn't mean you have to know all the answers. What it does give you is a level of understanding that is hard to mimic. Operational experts care specifically about the customer group they are working with; they have a passion for the role and/or sector, and for making a difference.

In a time where services are stretched, team members often don't see each other for weeks. One-to-ones with managers/supervisors are often needs-led, so they're focused on caseload rather than the professional's current need to have the space to explore, debrief and grow. This is why values are so important to the methodology and not merely the fourth element of the Training 4 Influence method.

For our facilitators, delivering the learning objectives is important and truly meeting the needs of the people in the room are even more so. These frontline professionals are literally keeping our criminal justice, social care and charity services going, changing lives despite the current political and austerity landscape. They are the superheroes, and alongside the planned session outcomes, some need recognition, support and re-motivating, while others need guidance, a values base and direction.

This is why it's so important to the delivery of the Training 4 Influence methodology to be an opera-tional expert who can walk the walk as well as talk the talk and relate to the experiences of the delegates on the courses. But is this enough on its own?

Some people subscribe to the view that being an expert makes you a great trainer; that operational expertise trumps everything else when it comes to helping peo-ple to learn. If you know your subject well, you can teach it to anyone, right?

And yet, think back to teachers you had at school. Let's assume that they were all equally knowledgeable about their subject. Even so, you probably regarded some as better teachers than others and enjoyed their classes more. What was it that set the good ones apart from the others? The answer is how they delivered the material to you, how they engaged with you.

The same goes for great speakers who can entertain an audience and hold people's attention with their knowledge of a subject. But that communication tends to be mainly one way, so it doesn't automatically follow that they'll be great facilitators.

Being an operational expert isn't enough. Although it's an important part of the Training 4 Influence method, it doesn't make you a great teacher or facilitator. It's not just about knowing your subject matter inside and out, and explaining or showing it to other people, even in an interesting way. It's about inspiring people to perform at their best, engaging them in their own learning and facilitating a shared journey – and that comes down to a different set of skills.

If you're already working in a training role, it's likely that you have facilitation skills in pretty good supply. But if you're not, there's no reason to think you can't be a great facilitator too. You don't need to have a background in training to become a great facilitator, but you must have some of the basic skills required by facilitators, and you must have the ability to acquire advanced facilitation skills quickly. For either a freelance or internal trainer, facilitation skills are necessary to engage delegates through the Training 4 Influence method.

I don't say this to put pressure on you, but because it's essential. I've seen what can happen when an operational expert doesn't have the facilitation skills to deliver a course. They tend to deliver the material in a dry way and important information can be lost as delegates switch off.

All the components of the Training 4 Influence methodology must be woven seamlessly together, and that's why you need to be both an operational expert *and* a great facilitator (or become one as quickly as you can). If you're not an operational expert, you'll lack credibility. You won't understand all the issues faced by delegates or how to help them most effectively. If you don't have facilitation skills, you won't be able to run courses to get the best out of delegates, generate discussions or make the sessions engaging.

The skills of the facilitator

'Tell me and I forget, teach me and I may remember, involve me and I learn.'
— Benjamin Franklin

Learning through involvement is what we want our facilitators to achieve. It's the winning combination of operational expertise and advanced facilitation skills that maximises the opportunity for learning, for light-bulb moments, for behaviour change.

We want facilitators to have qualities that we can build on. As a minimum requirement, these are the essential attributes a facilitator needs:

- Excellent communication skills

- Active listening skills

- A talent for questioning

- Great self-awareness and emotional intelligence

- A passion for learning and sharing knowledge

- The ability to give feedback in a constructive way

- A genuine interest in people, coupled with empathy

- Confidence and ease when presenting in front of an audience

- The ability to recognise and respond to delegates' needs

- The ability to think on their feet

- The ability to coach and motivate delegates

- The ability to collaborate with co-facilitators

Let's look at these important skills and attributes in more detail.

Excellent communication skills

It's absolutely vital that facilitators have the ability to explain ideas and concepts so that they're understood. This is not just about the words they use; it's about the pace and tone, the nuances of their delivery and the non-verbal communication, including facial expressions and gestures.

Excellent communication skills cover:

- Having the ability to adapt your communication to suit the subject and the group of delegates you're working with to help them learn. This could include slowing things down or explaining things in a different way, and doing this from an unbiased perspective so that you're not leading delegates to a pre-planned conclusion. Instead, you're genuinely seeking and encouraging opinions and ideas, which the group, or you and the delegate in a one-to-one situation, then discuss in a respectful, constructive and productive way.

- Building connection and mutual understanding.

- Having the ability to draw out quiet delegates or quieten dominant ones in a tactful and diplomatic way, while maintaining a positive and productive atmosphere.

Effective facilitators recognise the power of storytelling in maintaining engagement and illustrating points in ways that resonate with delegates and enhance the learning experience. If you can tell a story from your own journey, that motivates delegates to share their experiences, increasing the opportunities for discussion and debate.

Active listening skills

This is about the facilitator:

- Having the ability to listen intently to hear what isn't being said, as well as what is

- Being able to work out the needs of delegates, even when they may not be consciously aware of those needs themselves

- Hearing the explicit and implicit meaning of words

- Repeating and summing up what's been said, to ensure they have correctly understood the delegates and / or the delegates have correctly understood them

A talent for questioning

Effective facilitators are adept at using different types of questions to encourage open discussion and debate, and they value the contributions of delegates. They recognise the power of collaborative learning, rather than the traditional teacher role where the trainer leads discussions and provides answers.

An experienced facilitator recognises that there is a great opportunity for learning when facilitation is shared, from time to time, with other members of the group, and focuses on the goal of encouraging the most effective discussion. They know when to bring a discussion to a close, when to change topic, when to move the discussion away from someone who is dominating the rest of the group, when to let the discussion run over and when to use silence to elicit a response. They know how to use questioning to encourage engagement because they recognise that this is the best way to help learners learn.

Delegates need the opportunity to ask and answer questions, share and discuss views, and put into practice what they've learned. They also need to feel safe to share their concerns, fears, hopes and feelings. Effective facilitators foster an active and safe learning environment by using clear leadership and boundaries.

Great self-awareness and emotional intelligence

The best facilitators are aware of their own thoughts, emotions and behaviours. They know when they might be triggered by something and have coping strategies to help them maintain balance. Understanding how their own words and behaviours might impact others, they think carefully about how to express themselves. They self-assess their own performance and welcome feedback from others on their facilitation and their training materials, so that they can develop further as a facilitator.

A passion for learning and sharing knowledge

It stands to reason that the people who make the best facilitators are those who never lose their passion for learning. You have to keep learning if you want to remain an operational expert, but it's also important to *want* to do so. And it's critical to success that you have a real desire to help other people learn, too, by sharing your knowledge and experience, and by facilitating the course in such a way as to motivate delegates to learn more.

The ability to give feedback in a constructive way

Bearing in mind that the people who attend training courses may be struggling in their roles, either with their caseloads or with their wellbeing, or maybe both, facilitators need constructive dialogue to facilitate the learning process. It's really important that you're able to provide feedback to delegates in a way that is both encouraging and motivating, helping them to do their roles better rather than leaving them feeling worse about themselves.

A genuine interest in people, coupled with empathy

If you're a facilitator who is already working in the criminal justice, social care or charity sector, the chances are that you have plenty of empathy and a genuine interest in people. It would be hard to do your job if you didn't. That interest and empathy has to extend into the learning environment to get the best outcomes for your delegates. And what's more, you need to show your delegates that you want to understand their situation and the pressures they face. That's how you build rapport with them, because, after all, you are not the expert at being them.

Confidence and ease when presenting in front of an audience

Before becoming a facilitator, you need to have a basic level of confidence in your ability to speak in public, and not find yourself wishing the ground would open up and swallow you every time you stand up and take the podium. If the thought of speaking in front of groups makes you a bit nervous, your confidence will grow the more you do it. If the thought of standing up in front of groups makes you feel ill, then facilitation might not be your thing.

The ability to recognise and respond to delegates' needs

This is such an important aspect of the facilitator's role. You need to be able to recognise individual and group learning, along with other needs which may not be presented at first or may change as the course progresses. This is about being insightful and sensitive to the feelings of individuals and the group as a whole.

To build and maintain an atmosphere of trust, respect and openness, you need to be aware of factors, such as different cultural backgrounds and different levels of experience and confidence. You need to be able to recognise how people are responding to the topic and the views of others, and anyone who is either becoming emotional or withdrawing from discussions. On top of that, you need to pick up on the group chemistry in the same way and respond accordingly. This skilful facilitation requires a lot of empathy.

The ability to think on their feet

No matter how well prepared a facilitator is, each group they work with will be different to the last, and each individual will be different to the people sitting next to them. There's always scope for discussions not to proceed in the way you may have expected them to, or for someone to throw in a curveball.

A great facilitator has the ability to think on their feet, bring things back to the agenda, or take a slightly different path in mid-stream. This might involve using creative approaches to keep the group engaged, or taking ideas from the group to make the shift.

Always have a bag of tools that you can dip into to keep things moving and on track, even if there is a temporary detour. This means not losing sight of what the goal of the training is and referring back to the objectives if required. Also, know when to let people go off track, for example to clarify something, and when to bring things back to the main subject. Finally, acknowledge it when you don't have all the answers.

The ability to coach and motivate delegates

A great facilitator knows how to manage group dynamics to get the best out of delegates. This means sometimes having to deal with difficult situations, such as someone being triggered by a topic that's being discussed, conflict between delegates or someone struggling with their resilience.

As a facilitator, you need to know how to coach and motivate delegates to work with customers in a positive and realistic way by helping them to rediscover or reinforce their why. It's important to stress here that you need to value delegates embarking on their own learning journey. A great facilitator walks alongside them, rather than leading the way.

The ability to collaborate with co-facilitators

Where facilitators are working in pairs, they each need the ability to work well with their partner. It's important that contributions are balanced between them, they prepare equally, don't undermine one another and provide mutual support.

CHAPTER TOP TIPS

Facilitation:

- Learn what facilitation is and what it isn't.
- Be well prepared, but not afraid to change the plan if needed.
- Learn from more experienced facilitators.
- Know and value your strengths, and be honest with yourself about your areas for development.
- Keep learning new methods, tools and techniques.
- Encourage participation from the group and keep the energy flowing.
- Mix things up in the session so you're using different learning techniques (see Chapter 3).
- Use inclusive language in your sessions.

Being an operational expert:

- Look around at other people who deliver in the same subject area as you and whom you regard as experts. Ask yourself how your knowledge compares.
- Don't try to profess to know everything about everything. The delegates will see straight through you if you do.
- If possible, continue to work in the field alongside delivering training.
- Follow sectorial updates, themes and thought leaders on the internet to ensure you stay current.

- Undertake further study, particularly in new theory and legislation related to the topic.
- Shadow someone in their role.
- Talk to your delegates. Ask for practical examples of the work they do (more on this in Chapter 3).

If you don't have operational experience and need to deliver good training, recognise that you still have the ability to do so while valuing the contributions of delegates. In this case, having a co-facilitator who has worked in the area and/or with the customer group, or a couple of guest speakers to relate the topic to the delegates and their customer group, will add an important dimension to your training.

3
Tailored

How many times have you found yourself on a training course where the subject matter was relevant to you, but the examples used weren't? Maybe you were asked to look at a case example that was set in a completely different sector, with no relevance to your work at all. Perhaps the trainer discussed legislation not linked to the principles and practices in your setting.

The training may have met its learning objectives, but not yours. You may have gained information you can take back to your role, but the learning experience won't have been as intense as it could have if the activities and explanations had been relevant to you. And this can make it hard to learn and retain the information. Being able to link what you're learning back to your role is what prompts the a-ha moments where lightbulbs switch on in your head and things fall into place.

Over the course of my education and career, I've spent too much time on training sessions where it was important for me to learn what was being taught, but the examples didn't resonate with me. They all felt like missed opportunities.

If the examples had been tailored to my sector and role, the experience would have been rich with learning and so much more beneficial. It would have helped me to remember the why behind what I was doing, which would have meant my organisation reaped a much greater return on the time and money it had invested in me.

One of the key things we do at Taye is to tailor our training so that every aspect of the course resonates with every individual attending it. This chapter sets out to explain how to tailor your training to the relevant sector, organisation, team and individual to ensure you achieve the biggest impact possible. But first, an overview of why it's so essential to keep your knowledge and your courses up to date.

Staying relevant

> 'Continuous improvement is better than delayed perfection.'
> — Mark Twain

The criminal justice, social care and charity sectors are in crisis. For organisations, this means they don't meet their mission or operate in line with their values. They get poor quality assurance results and, aside from the potentially devastating impact on staff and customers, are at risk of real and lasting reputational damage.

There are pinch points everywhere. It's like the game where blocks of wood are removed one by one from a tower, putting a strain on the remaining blocks, until eventually the whole thing comes crashing down.

If a training solution is tailored to an organisation, it can make changes at an individual level so that the organisation doesn't go into crisis. It strengthens the sum of all the parts that make up an organisation. In other words, it helps to fortify the foundations to make the tower more stable.

None of us can change the charity, criminal justice and social care landscape. What we can do is use Training 4 Influence to help to change things for marginalised and vulnerable people, and vulnerable staff too.

If you're delivering a course, people have come to you either to learn something new, for a refresher, or to be updated on current changes. Therefore, the session needs to be grounded in legislation, best practice and guidance.

Unfortunately, this isn't always the case.

CASE EXAMPLE

One of Taye's facilitators, who is a local authority manager, told me recently how he attended mandatory training as part of his induction and the information was out of date. He mentioned it to the facilitator at the break, and the facilitator said he only had a few more sessions to deliver, and then the course content would be due its annual review.

The Taye facilitator was shocked. This approach quite simply isn't good enough. Things change and they change fast, and if people are paying a facilitator to deliver a course, they are perfectly within their rights to expect the most up-to-date version.

If we as facilitators share the current legislative position and best practice and guidance, delegates feel more empowered in their roles and are equipped with the tools and knowledge to deliver effectively. Delegates on training courses are typically time poor, so will tend to file e-mails with briefings of changes to read later, or maybe even delete them. Facilitators are in a privileged position – we have the undivided attention of our delegates for hours at a time. They deserve the best we can offer them.

Another key aspect of Training 4 Influence is ensuring that our course content is informed by the legislation, guidance and best practice relevant to both the sector and the activities of the organisation that we're working with. We don't just want our training to be good, we want it to be the best.

Whatever sector you work in, it's vital for people to be operating within the laws and codes of practice that exist. It's the role of the facilitator to make sure that all training is absolutely accurate in its delivery of legislative information. In addition to this, best practice and guidance are extremely helpful for a facilitator; they can even transform the way we deliver our services. If someone developed a new method, learned lessons after a serious incident or conducted research to show a better, more impactful way of delivering services, you'd want to know – right?

Layering

'Quality is never an accident. It is always the result of intelligent effort.'
— John Ruskin

This method strand is multi-dimensional, taking into consideration numerous things. The political background can drive reform and uncertainty. Nothing ever stands still in our world, so there are ongoing legislation and guidance changes. Quality assurers change their expectations; local authorities change their requirements; and serious case reviews bring forth important lessons to take into consideration.

When I write a course on a specific subject, relevant to a specific sector, I consider the things it must include step by step. I like to think of it as layering.

The first layer is legislation and legislative guidance. What laws (if any) govern the course you are developing and what laws have influence or connection? Legislation often provides the bedrock of training sessions, particularly mandatory training.

As Taye often covers issues that are guided or mandated by legislation, it's crucial that as facilitators, we remain as up to date as we can possibly be. In fact, at Taye we see it as a fundamental part of our service to update organisations on changes to legislation so that they don't have to strive to be on top of everything themselves.

This means building legislative changes into our courses. It also means horizon-scanning to be aware of consultations that are underway and what the likely outcomes are, so that we can share this information with delegates to forewarn them of the direction of travel.

Legislation and guidance will vary according to the course that a facilitator is delivering. Your aim needs to be to deliver on what is key and relevant. Guidance is often published soon after new legislation to explain the detail in a more understandable, applicable way. Helpfully, this guidance often interprets the legislation for different sectors and situations, so you can utilise case examples and references from the guidance to inform your activities.

Staying up to date is not just about being aware that new legislation and guidance is coming into force or has been enacted, though. It's also about following where issues arise. There are often areas of contention or grey areas that can be interpreted (or misinterpreted) in a number of ways. Having a comprehensive knowledge of legislation means understanding it at a strategic level and how it impacts on professional practice on the ground. It also means being able to keep abreast of case law development and understanding what these developments mean for the practical application of the law, making those connections for delegates so they don't have to.

Of course, this aspect is ever-changing and never ending, as new pieces of legislation and guidance come into force. The key thing is to make sure that delegates on your courses learn everything they need to know about the legislation and guidance that's relevant to their roles.

This can be a source of stress and complexity for an organisation, particularly on the frontline. Often operational professionals hold the view that they spend too much time completing paperwork and not enough time with their customers. In all our sessions, we reframe the rationale for quality assurance and monitoring. It is about ensuring the customer receives a quality service, with the best possible chance of a positive outcome. The evidence collated to highlight this helps a service to be recommissioned or an organisation become more successful when applying for new services or funding. Monitoring and quality assurance can also help focus people in busy times, ensuring a crucial element of a service isn't missed because their focus is elsewhere.

If, like Taye, all your training is connected to frontline practice, the second layer may be to look at certain standards and expectations in detail when you're developing a course. For us, these include:

- Ofsted

- The Charity Commission

- National Commissioners

- Quality Assurance Framework

- The Care Quality Commission

- Ministry of Justice

If we as facilitators take the time to consider monitoring and quality assurance when we are writing and tailoring courses, we offer much better value to the customer, as they can be reassured that the training will meet the standards they need. If useful, we even provide the evidence they need to report. This could be as simple as the number of delegates who have attended the course for a specific report request.

I refer to this element as layering as there is so much information to consider if you are truly going to provide the best learning experience. It isn't always the detail of the information, but its applicability to the roles of the delegates attending that's important.

The third layer is additional information, such as:

- Inspection reports
- National Institute for Clinical Excellence (NICE) guidance
- New academic best practice
- Serious case reviews
- Bills going through parliament
- Articles, talks and other information from leaders in the area of work

Facilitators have to be knowledgeable about the standards that apply, the changing expectations of quality assurers, recommendations from reports, lessons learned and serious case reviews.

How does this all connect together? Let's use safeguarding as an example again. The Children's Act mandates the safeguarding response, but local authorities can determine their own thresholds and expectations. A training facilitator has to know both the content of the act and the local variances.

It can be a complex area. This diagram illustrates the layering we take into consideration at Taye when developing our course content.

Taye Course Content Determinants

As a training company, Taye applies for our courses to be independently accredited. CPD is an accreditation of the quality of delivery, not content.

We CPD accredit all our core courses for two reasons. Firstly, it role models the importance of external scrutiny. Secondly, some of our delegates need to achieve a certain number of CPD points annually to retain their professional accreditation.

CPD signifies a commitment made by professionals to enhance their personal skills and proficiency throughout their careers. It describes a range of learning activities that give people the opportunity to develop and consolidate their skills, knowledge and experience, and it ensures that people who qualify in a particular subject continue to learn so that their knowledge remains current and their skills are continually updated. Then no one becomes rusty or operates based on out-of-date knowledge. Not only that, it provides people with opportunities to add to their skills.

If these opportunities are provided through a CPD accredited route, that means delegates either reach or exceed the CPD standards for quality and integrity, following scrutiny and assessment by the CPD Certification Service. In a nutshell, that means the training is clear, meets its objectives and delivers training of an accredited quality.

It also means that the training includes vocational and skills-based or practical learning. Whatever sector you work in, meeting industry standards and knowing what changes are 'just around the corner' is a must. When you are working in an organisation that is delivering life-changing services, having the most recent information can be the difference between advocating effectively and meeting the needs of your customer, or not.

Because Taye delivers both specialist courses that have been developed at the request of an organisation, and standard core courses which are usually presented either as part of a general induction or as a refresher, they can vary significantly.

The layering process is exactly the same for all courses, whether core or specialist courses, but the detail, guidance, legislation and best practice available can vary hugely. For instance, core skills training will cover subjects such as safeguarding, risk management, managing challenging behaviours, the Mental Capacity Act, equality and diversity, professional boundaries and lone working. All of these have an absolute abundance of information to consider, but the picture can be quite different when we develop and deliver specialist sessions.

An example of a specialist course could be one that covers areas such as disguised compliance (where parents or carers *appear* to be co-operating with service providers to avoid arousing suspicions and risking action being taken against them), working with people convicted of sexual offences, or first responder for receptionists. There may be some connected legislation or guidance and we may be able to find some academic research or best practice, but there isn't an abundance.

Usually quality assurers aren't even aware specialist courses are needed; the request for them comes from operational needs rather than a monitoring require-ment. The facilitator still undertakes the same steps, though, to ensure that the course delivers as much as it possibly can.

Aim to provide training where the subject matter is clear, the objectives robust and the sessions exceed industry quality standards. Quite simply, use Training 4 Influence to create the next generation of operational experts and help those currently in a role to stay on top of their game. That's not big-headed; it's about wanting to do the best that you can to deliver training that fully meets the needs of the sector.

Legislation is vitally important

'Legislation should be the voice of reason.'
— Pythagoras of Samos

When work is full on and there never seems to be enough hours in the day, keeping on top of legislative and best practice changes can be difficult. If you're inexperienced, you might not want to bother your more experienced colleagues with questions. If you're experienced, you might not want to admit that you don't know the answers. And all the while, things change, sometimes daily.

But staying up to date on these issues is a key aspect of effective delivery, and an essential part of being the person who makes a difference to someone's life. And as facilitators, we have a duty to do our bit to lighten the load of those at the sharp end.

Taye's rationale for considering legislation, best practice and guidance isn't just to tick a box; it's to inform daily activity. Legislation has to be operated within, whether we agree with it or not.

To deliver the most effective services to our delegates, we as facilitators need to know the legislative limitations to the services they can access, how best to advocate for them, the funding they are eligible for, the impact of the behaviours they are displaying. Having this knowledge to hand enables us to advise and guide our delegates more effectively in how to deliver services, respond in different circumstances and save lives.

We must never forget that our training is delivered to professionals working with complex and/or vulnerable people. The world is constantly turning, and we owe it to these professionals to know whether someone has found a more effective way of undertaking a task or developed a new tool, skill or intervention.

Tailoring training

The layering forms the skeleton of the course, following legislation, best practice and guidance, but for the course to really make a difference, it also needs to be tailored to the particular organisation, team and customer group. This means a personalised level of service.

The initial contact with an organisation (or department or team) is a facilitator's opportunity to begin to get to know their prospective customer, so its importance shouldn't be underestimated. It's about the customer, not about the facilitator.

If, as facilitators, we can 'get' our customer and their organisation, it gives us the opportunity to deliver a first-class product that will ensure a great learning experience and leave delegates hungry for more. Without doing this groundwork, we'll only ever be able to deliver something fairly generic that won't fully hit the mark.

The same applies to in-house training providers working with internal customers. Even though you know the organisation well, you still need to really understand the requirements of the specific teams and contextualise them to deliver something truly valuable.

The initial contact

Perhaps, when an enquiry comes in, you ask a few questions about the type of training the organisation is interested in, who the organisation is and the work it does. Then you sign off by promising to send some information.

It would be really simple if it happened like that, but it wouldn't fully deliver what the organisation needs. Nor would it provide the high-quality training that we all need to build our reputations on as facilitators. You can't deliver that quality if you don't know much about the organisation, its customers and its potential delegates.

There is certain key information you need to request during the initial contact:

- Why is the organisation booking the training?

- Who will be attending (roles, responsibilities, etc)?

- What is the organisation's current operating context (customers, geography, services)?

- What are its mission, vision, values, aims, objectives and challenges?

It's not just about making a sale or ticking a box; it's about building a picture, a tapestry of the organisation and its employees' needs. Is there a knowledge gap, or has there been an issue that has highlighted a need for training? Is it for new recruits? Is it as a result of legislative reforms? And who are the organisation's customers? What kind of services do they need and what issues are they facing?

You then use this information to weave a thread through everything the organisation's representative has told you. As you build the picture, you can link critical parts together to create your training magic.

Writing the proposal

Once you've gathered all the information from the initial contact, it's time to write the proposal, setting out the offering, which will incorporate the brief you've been given during the call/meeting. This is usually a short document, attached to which is the booking form. As an in-house provider, you may not need to write a proposal unless you need approval at a higher level, and I can't imagine you would be using a booking form.

For those who do need to write a proposal, the key is to start with an overview of the brief that was given. Reflect the discussion you've had about the mission, visions and values, and any specific tailoring that the organisation's representative has requested. This is your opportunity to set out how the brief will be not just met, but exceeded, and how the training you propose will deliver real value, not just on the requested subject, but also on wider related matters.

For example, if there have been practice and quality assurance issues, there may also be team dynamic or morale issues. The aim of the session will be to provide training not just on the immediate issue, but on underlying or latent issues which need to be addressed to provide a complete solution. Don't just look at the parts of the situation; look at the whole.

Then look at the number and length of the training sessions. Is the proposal for a one-day session, two half-day sessions, two days taking place several weeks apart? This will depend on the overall aims of the training and the associated content, and whether there is a need for some consolidation or other work to take place between sessions.

After that, headline the content of each session. This provides information on what you plan to cover at a high level to enable the organisation to see if the content meets its needs. You should also say if the course has been CPD accredited.

It's also helpful to include some information about you as the trainer/facilitator and why you are the best person to deliver these sessions at this proposal point, including any specific experience or qualifications. If you have completed the Training 4 Influence course you would add our accreditation logo and information about how your training delivers added influence. At Taye Training, because we have multiple facilitators, we often share the methodology and accreditations at the proposal level and the facilitator details when the booking form is received.

Finally, detail the price. Be specific here about what is included and anything that is not, so the organisation's representative knows exactly what value they will get for their investment. And don't forget to include the booking form. You can find an example proposal document and booking form to download on the Taye website at: https://training4influence. co.uk/resources/

If you've understood the brief properly and reflected that in the proposal, you should see a high positive response rate.

When the booking form is sent back

The return of the booking forms signals a commitment to work together. If you're an in-house provider, the commitment to proceed may simply come in the form of an email, phone call or other agreement.

When you start working with an organisation (or team/department), ask your contact which bodies and guidance they need you to reference. For example, at Taye, we ask charities which commissioners they work with, so that we know the expectations and standards and what's mandated.

In addition, there will often be local expectations to meet, too. When you are tailoring a course, it's important to ask about this, as different localities have hugely different expectations.

Once an organisation has given its commitment, ask its representative for more information. This will not only be useful in designing the detail of the course, but also help with dynamics on the day. At this stage, focus on gathering as much additional information as you can. I would usually do this by having a phone call, ideally with an operational manager who has knowledge and experience of the subject matter, but it may be with someone from the organisation's HR team. It doesn't matter if it's the latter, as you can pick up on specific operational matters in more detail later on.

To be clear, it should be the person who will facilitate the event who makes the call. My normal practice with Taye would be to make the final decision on the facilitator once the booking has been confirmed. The facilitator is matched to the organisation based on the information I've received, the training required and each facilitator's experience. Then I'll tell the organisation why I made the match.

There is an important reason for the facilitator making the call to the organisation. It builds trust and rapport, and gives the representative faith that the facilitator understands their organisation's issues, which enables a different type of conversation to take place.

It also means that the facilitator has a clear view of the organisation, its operating context and any existing or latent issues.

The first thing you want to do (or your facilitator wants to do) is understand in more detail why the organisation is looking for training. Why did its representative choose you and what are their overarching objectives? Information from the organisation may be limited at this stage as you haven't established a close working relationship yet, but by doing your own research, you can build up quite a detailed picture.

As well as speaking to your contact within the organisation, spend time looking at the organisation's website to get as much understanding as you can of what it does, who its people are, how and why they operate, and what they want to achieve. Make sure you understand who their customer groups are to get a picture of the kind of issues they might be facing.

Ask your contact to send any connected policies; you may well be asked to review and update these as part of developing the training. Why is this important? The answer is that training and policies are inextricably linked. The policies underpin the training and vice-versa. If a policy doesn't adequately cover a situation or gives incorrect information, it can leave staff members exposed. If the content of a policy and the content of a training session are different, it can lead to confusion and inconsistency of practice.

Let's use lone working as an example. If the policy details one process for recording risk and the training uses another, this could lead to different parts of the organisation doing different things, which can create conflict and lead to inconsistency, resulting in unsafe practices.

After your initial information-gathering phase, wait until around one month prior to the training taking place before getting in touch with the organisation again. This time, ensure you speak with an operational manager or some of the attendees to get the operational background to the training request.

Asking about the wider benefits the organisation wants to achieve usually opens the door to a more open and frank discussion about exactly what issues it would like addressed. This allows you to develop a training course that is going to add significant value to the organisation, because the content will be appropriately tailored to its employees' specific requirements. The information you get will enable you to identify suitable activities based on delegates' needs and values.

Learning about the delegates ahead of the training adds another important dimension. It allows you to understand the pressures at more than an organisational level. You can build up knowledge of where the pinch points might be at a team and individual level, which helps you to make the training even more relevant to the current operating context. It also allows you to build up an understanding of the impacts that lack of funding, demand for services and customers with complex needs are having on the team and individuals.

Creating the course

Once you've obtained this information, you can develop the course. Some courses will be written from scratch, while others will already have been formed, but you can tailor them to suit the organisation's particular needs.

For example, if the course is for an organisation which works with young people, remove case studies that relate to adults with dementia. Likewise, if it is a care organisation, take out case studies that relate to working with substance misuse. Every aspect needs to be tailored, including all of the activities.

CASE EXAMPLE

This case example involves what's called an approved premises. This is a place for people who have just been released from prison (who are deemed to be high risk) to go to, rather than returning immediately to the community.

All the residents within this particular approved premises were males with personality disorders. The approved premises was located in a city centre, which made it difficult to manage the group and, on top of this, there were issues of inconsistency of practice from the staff team because of the dynamics of the situation.

The team manager contacted me to ask for some assertiveness training for the staff team. Through questioning, I established that the team was made up of some relatively inexperienced young staff who were struggling with the group. The group, on the other hand, knew the system well and many had been in approved premises before. The staff were low paid, working shifts, had little training and turnover was high. Furthermore, the staff team didn't like one another and blamed each other for the problems that existed. They hadn't bonded, so there was no mutual support. Actually, the team was close to breaking down.

I knew that rolling out assertiveness training on its own wouldn't have the desired effect. The team needed to reconnect with one another. Their professional boundaries were slipping. For example, they weren't maintaining the curfew, which was a big issue when you consider that the men had restrictions applied to their release. The men themselves recognised which members of the team were weaker and who could be taken advantage of.

Once I'd gathered all of this information, I did some research into approved premises, assertiveness training, professional boundaries and team building. From this, I produced a proposal that comprised of these topics:

- Team building
- Professional boundaries

- Managing difficult conversations
- Assertiveness

The proposal was accepted, and the next call that took place was between the Taye facilitator and the manager to find out more about the team dynamics. What were the strengths and weaknesses of the team? Who would support the training, who would push against it?

We learned of issues that had arisen and found out exactly what the manager was worried about and what the aim was. This resulted in training that focused on the three specific topics I suggested, with lots of team building activities woven throughout to reconnect the staff. The three topics were:

- Professional boundaries
- Managing difficult conversations
- Assertiveness

Professional boundaries was chosen as the first topic because these were being compromised, so reinforcing them made it easier for the other topics to be addressed. All the policies were woven into the training.

During the training, delegates were purposely moved around so they all had the chance to work together. The team moved from giving each other grief to laughing and joking with each other.

The final activity the facilitator used with the team is called the Circle of Concern, first introduced by Stephen Covey in his influential book *The 7 Habits of Highly Effective People*.[2] This is an incredibly powerful

---

2   S R Covey, *The 7 Habits of Highly Effective People: Powerful lessons in personal change,* (The Free Press, fifteenth anniversary edition, 2004)

tool to use. It involves delegates putting their concerns and barriers in a box on the table at the beginning of the course, then at the end of the course, the whole group works through them one by one, without saying who wrote down each concern. The concerns are then plotted on a Circle of Concern/Circle of Influence, with the whole group identifying tools from the training course that they could use to influence and overcome each concern.

By the end of the session, the delegates had been honest about which concerns they had written and why. They were now more confident about sharing their true feelings with their colleagues and asking for support.

The feedback from the course was phenomenal, and the facilitator was able to see immediate tangible results during the course with people changing their practice in front of her eyes.

Get into the detail

This is a crucial stage because it is where you have the opportunity to give some real benefits to organisations that can have the power to transform teams and service delivery. In addition to ensuring that the course is written to consider legislation, best practice and the organisation's policies, ask who its quality assurers are and maybe ask to be sent the connected elements. This will ensure the organisation gets the best possible value from your training.

It's also of the utmost importance to remember how crucial language is. If you use language that delegates identify with, they feel more connected to the training and have more faith in you as a facilitator. For example, calling someone a service user may not sit well with some organisations. Have a conversation with your point of contact at the organisation to identify their preferred terminology and identify terms that may cause issues with their customer groups.

Words can calm a situation, or they can inflame it. Words can support someone, or inflict damage. Words can convey a different meaning from what you intended. 'Careless talk costs lives' was a slogan during the Second World War. This is an apt phrase for the potential impact of the wrong language on vulnerable people. Not all examples of using inappropriate language are going to lead to a catastrophic outcome, but nevertheless, they can set the wrong tone for a discussion with someone.

For example, calling someone a sex offender is a reminder of the worst thing they have done, so it may be more appropriate to refer to them as a person who has committed a sexual offence. It may be more appropriate to call a vulnerable adult an adult at risk, or to call a young offender a young person who has committed a crime. The differences may seem subtle to you, but not so much to the person on the receiving end of what can be seen as a negative label.

CASE EXAMPLE

Recently, I watched a video of children in care talking about language used to refer to them that they don't like. This included 'looked-after child', which makes them feel like they don't belong, that they are a ward of the system. They also don't like the term 'placement', because this feels formal and cold. They prefer to be told: 'This is going to be your home for a while'. Certain language makes them feel devalued and that they really don't matter.

Language is such a powerful thing that I really don't subscribe to the old saying 'Sticks and stones may break my bones, but names will never hurt me'. We can inflict so much damage with the language we use and it can have a long-lasting impact, so put a lot of effort in to making sure that you get your language right. In training situations, I find it is best to ask people what terminology they prefer to hear and see to help prevent barriers.

If I'm using an existing course, I'll work through the content and amend it to make sure it's relevant to the organisation I'm about to work with. I'll insert some slides showing the organisation's mission and values, and I'll ensure I know enough about the delegates to connect them to the course content. (Some example slides are available at https://training4influence. co.uk/resources/.) I will also ask them for some case examples and the appropriate forms of language to use in the activities, which helps to ensure the session is relevant to the organisation's aims and customers. Then I find out the organisation's quality assurers and make sure the content exceeds their standards, is written with reference to the organisation's internal policies, and reflects current legislation and best practice.

This may seem like a lot of work, but it takes approximately 60–90 minutes, including the phone call and the tailoring of the course, to ensure it is relevant. If you are going to be delivering the same course multiple times, the time you need to tailor the course lessens for each occasion, with the only repeatable extra being to ensure that you have an understanding of how the delegates may differ.

Taye's courses only exist because an organisation asked us to develop them. If we have an expert with the right experience, we are happy to do this. We then market the course for others to purchase and tailor it accordingly. This means that although similar learning objectives are being met the course may present quite differently.

You may develop completely bespoke courses. If you do, all of the advice we've covered in this section holds true, with some subtle additions. These can best be demonstrated through an example.

CASE EXAMPLE

I was approached by an organisation that wanted training for reception staff who were dealing with customers with addictions. The organisation described the need as training in basic customer-care skills, handling telephone calls, being aware of body language and tone, and content of verbal communications. This need had arisen because reception staff were not dealing appropriately with customers and were, in some cases, being unhelpful, treating them as if they were worthless – or at least, that was the perception of those on the receiving end.

The organisation representative was honest about their motives for booking the training; they explained that they felt some of the issues were so serious, they might require disciplinary action. At the time, the staff could use lack of training as a defence against disciplinary action, so introducing training would remove that excuse if there were further instances of poor customer service. But the organisation also wanted to support people to deliver the right level of service. It wanted the course to recognise the principle of duty of candour and how it applies to a team situation (ie that people can take responsibility for their actions without taking personal responsibility).

We identified actual objectives for the course. The way that customers were being treated was a by-product of the team issues, so the objectives had to change to focus on resolving these issues to the benefit of team members and the customers they were serving. With input from the organisation, the objectives were broken down into:

- Rebuilding the team
- Changing the culture
- Reigniting customer-service skills
- Developing different ways of working
- Building the team's confidence when working with the customers

We changed the title of the course from Customer Service to First Responders. There was a real chance that calling the course by the former title would have got the delegates' backs up before it had even started, as it wasn't a case of them not having the necessary customer-service skills.

In developing the course, I made sure that it was going to cover the delegates' journey into their role and their why behind doing what they do, to bring them back to what was important for them and what it was about the role that made them tick. A big feature of the course was crucial conversations, to reinforce the point that, when dealing with customers, the team members held the power. I included skills-building exercises to ensure confidence in approach.

It was important that the course impressed upon the delegates that their customers were not just those people who walked in the door, but their colleagues and any other stakeholders, too, so I developed a session that focused on how they could all work together as a team to be happier and provide an excellent service. This would allow them to feel appreciated as team members, to show their appreciation for one another, and to have the space to talk and reignite the skills they already had.

Happily, the outcome of all this work was a team that was much more cohesive and delivering a higher standard of customer care as a result, which wouldn't have been achieved if we had set out only to address the customer care aspects. Taye now has a first responder course which we deliver regularly to GP surgery or recovery receptionists and other people working on front desks.

The impact of taking the extra time to tailor a course is phenomenal. It can be the difference between the delegates understanding and retaining 20% or 80% of the content. It can change a session from being viewed as 'information we need to learn' to 'information that is vital for our role'. It can be the difference between a delegate feeling lectured and taught information to walking out of the session feeling valued, capable and motivated to continue delivering excellent services.

CHAPTER TOP TIPS

Tailoring your sessions:

- Sign up for government updates and follow thought leaders in the field.
- Don't overwhelm yourself with legislation. Related guidance is often the easier first read.
- Layer your courses. Go through the process step by step so you can be sure you have considered everything your delegates will need.
- Consider applicability. Slides with reams of legislation are not helpful; clear takeaways with an activity to embed the learning are much more effective.

- You do not need to know everything; you can signpost delegates towards further reading where appropriate.

Whether a course is developed from scratch or you're tailoring an existing course, there are some principles that hold true:

- Always ensure that you get clear goals or objectives for the course from both those arranging it and those who will be attending.

- Always consider the use of language. Remember different words mean different things to different people. This can be from a personal perspective and an organisational perspective.

- Weave activities into the training that will resonate with the group. One activity that I find really powerful is the continuum of concern.[3]

- Connect the session to the organisation's mission, vision and values.

- Ask to see relevant policies and weave them throughout the training session (where relevant), rather than just showing a slide about them.

- Consider the context the organisation you are delivering to works in. For instance, if you were writing a safeguarding-connected course for the National Health Service, you would ensure the course met Care Quality Commission standards and followed the intercollegiate guidance, but you wouldn't consider Ofsted or grant commissioners.

---

3   www.theproudtrust.org/digital-youth-work-hub/continuum-of-concern

4
Engaging

The pressure on organisations and individual members of staff in the statutory criminal justice, social care and charity sectors is immense. The painful irony is that as the pressure increases, organisations need to invest in more training to help their staff manage this situation, but they have less money nowadays to spend on equipping staff with the skills that they need.

It's increasingly important that training delivers the maximum impact possible to make budgets stretch further. That's why the Training 4 Influence methodology helps people to immerse themselves fully in training to increase the opportunity for learning.

As facilitators, we want people to leave our courses having enjoyed the whole experience and remained engaged and motivated throughout. We want to see light bulbs going on all over the place, and we want the delegates to take away as much learning as they can. When they retain that learning, they can apply it effectively in an operational setting. And we want them to feel confident about positively impacting on someone's life.

This chapter aims to show you how to make sure that every delegate gets the most out of the training you give, to maximise the opportunity for learning. It will set out two of the ways that you can do this: by taking account of individual learning styles and by using accelerated learning techniques to make your training as engaging and interactive as possible.

The importance of learning styles

'We think too much about effective methods of teaching and not enough about effective methods of learning.'
— John Carolus S J

One of the reasons Faye and I started Taye Training was our frustration about attending training courses that were the opposite of engaging and interactive. I'm sure you know what I mean: death by Power-Point. Some we were really excited to attend, but once we were there, we'd find our eyes slowly closing and our minds wandering while we planned our shopping lists in our head.

For a long time, I thought it was my fault that I didn't get the most from the training I received, particularly when I was at university in one lecture or seminar after another. My fault I couldn't concentrate; my fault I didn't retain the information; my fault that even though I was interested and excited by the subject, I was falling asleep. It made me wonder what was wrong with me.

Then my perspective changed. I love people-watching, and as I attended courses in my twenties and early thirties, I started looking around. I wasn't the only one whose eyes were rolling, whose head was drooping and who was gazing out of the window – about a third of each cohort was doing the same. In general terms, I have quite a good attention span; I can concentrate, get work done, but I can't just sit and listen. Not effectively, anyway.

When Faye and I started Taye Training, I did a lot of research into learning styles. I didn't want a third of our delegates to fall asleep. Giving up a day to be trained is precious time to them and they may not get that opportunity again for a while, so the sessions are important. The information is important – literally lifesaving in some cases.

The struggle that some people have to stay alert and retain information isn't anyone's fault. As individuals, we all learn differently. We all have a specific sense that helps us to stay alert and retain information, but physiologically, we are not made to sit for hours and hours listening to someone talk. We need to be engaged.

In addition to this, we have two types of intelligence: intellectual and emotional. In my experience of delivering hundreds of sessions, I've found that stimulating both these intelligences and ensuring that all learning styles are covered gives all participants equal opportunity to understand, process and retain the information. That's critical to the learning process.

What's also important is to speed up the learning process to allow people to take in and retain more information in a shorter space of time. There's a benefit for everyone in accelerating the process because learners learn more, facilitators can deliver more and organisations get more content and better outcomes. This is vital in the current climate.

Organisations often see that their staff are struggling in their roles. There is a real level of inexperience that they need to address, otherwise their experienced staff will sink under the strain. The pressure of work is causing issues with wellbeing and team dynamics. This is leading to problems with service delivery.

But organisations literally cannot afford to spend money on something that isn't going to deliver, or that only delivers to some of the delegates. They need training that's going to light a spark with every single person attending it and send them back to work refreshed and re-motivated.

You can do this in a number of ways, all of which are part of the Training 4 Influence methodology and are included in the expert, tailored and values chapters. However, it's also really important that the training is engaging and interactive and you tailor what you do to different learning styles. This takes the training up to a whole other level and produces amazing end results, which is what I want from each and every session that is run.

Have you ever talked to a friend or colleague about a training session after the event to discover that you found it engaging, whereas they found it dull? Or perhaps you remember growing frustrated in the past about not being able to learn a new practical skill as quickly as your friend, but you tended to understand new theories more easily than they did. That was probably down to different learning styles.

There has been lots of work done on the concept of learning styles over the years and each theory is, of course, different from the last one. One might resonate with you more than others. The important thing is that all the theories point to the fact that there *are* different learning styles, and that's the crucial bit for me. Where the theories differ is in what those styles are.

I don't subscribe to or advocate any one theory over another. My approach is to take the bits that resonate most with me and that have worked and continue to work best for me when I'm delivering training. And although most people have a preferred style, we all tend to use a mixture of some or all styles when we're learning something new, so I'd advise you to opt for variety in your training delivery. The key thing is to remember that people learn differently, and so the format of your sessions has to have variety to account for different preferences, speeds of learning, time for reflection, etc. This fits with the principles of accelerated learning.

Here is an overview of the main theories for those who haven't come across them before. Having knowledge of the theories enables you to tailor training to take into account the different ways in which people learn, enabling them to learn more effectively because they enjoy the experience so much more. (For more detail, go to https://training4influence.co.uk/resources/). The more that training is tailored to people's learning styles, the more effective it will be and the quicker people will learn, particularly when it's combined with accelerated learning. That's the Taye way.

Kolb's experiential learning

David A Kolb is possibly the name that most people associate with learning styles and theory. He developed the experiential learning theory, which aims to explain not just how people learn differently, but also that there is an experience we all go through when learning.[4]

He describes the four key stages of the learning cycle:

• You have an immediate or concrete experience

• This provides a basis for observations or reflection

• These are distilled into abstract concepts or theories

• These you actively test or experiment with to create new experiences

Imagine being a young child in the middle of winter, playing outside in the snow. You slide a few times (an immediate or concrete experience) and this leads you to observe that snow is slippery, and some areas are more slippery than others (observations and reflections). You then develop a theory that the areas where the snow has been compacted are more slippery (abstract concepts or theories) and you experiment

---

4   D A Kolb, *Experiential Learning: Experience as the source of learning and development* (Prentice Hall, 1984)

by sliding on different parts of the pavement to see which parts are the most slippery (actively testing).

In other words, you do something, you think about what has just happened, you work out why it's happened, and then you test out your theory. That's experiential learning in action.

Kolb's theory focused on four learning styles:

- Diverging (feeling and watching). These are people who prefer to look at things from different perspectives and watch, rather than do. They tend to gather information and use imagination to solve problems. They like working in groups, are interested in people and are open to other people's views.

- Assimilating (watching and thinking). These are people who prefer to take a logical approach and favour concepts over people. They love hearing and taking in lots of information that they can organise methodically and logically. Their preference is to listen to lectures, exploring theories and models and having time to think about them.

- Converging (doing and thinking). These are people who prefer to solve problems, particularly practical ones. They favour technical tasks over social or interpersonal issues, and love to experiment with new ideas to simulate and work with practical applications.

- Accommodating (doing and feeling). These people prefer to be 'hands-on' and use gut-feeling, rather than logic. They love new challenges and experiences, and prefer roles requiring practical action and initiative. They favour working in teams to complete tasks and meet targets.

What I find interesting about this theory is that it can be applied to how teams work together as much as it can apply to how people learn. Taking account of learning styles in a training session that is about rebuilding teams can have double the impact. If team members develop awareness of how their colleagues learn and why they behave as they do in a team situation, it serves to increase mutual understanding and strengthens working relationships.

According to Kolb, we have a preferred style which may change as we go through different stages in our development. If someone shows us a new piece of equipment for work, it would be socially unacceptable and probably quite career-limiting to learn about it by putting it in our mouths. But that's the way our much younger selves would have been likely to learn.

I like this concept of learning differently as we mature. Children tend to learn more instinctively and openly, but as we move through the education system and progress our working career, we are encouraged to learn differently, following the learning processes that have been set out for us and fit in with societal norms.

Honey and Mumford's learning styles

Peter Honey and Alan Mumford took Kolb's work and created a simplified version of the four learning styles.[5] This is possibly the best-known learning styles theory.

Honey and Mumford's learning styles are:

- Activist

- Reflector

- Theorist

- Pragmatist

These four styles effectively represent the four key stages of learning, as described by Kolb.

- Activists like to have an experience immediately. They tend to be open-minded and can get bored during implementation.

- Reflectors like to review the experience by standing back, gathering data, listening before

5   P Honey and A Mumford, *The Manual of Learning Styles* (Peter Honey, London 1982)

speaking and delaying decisions while they reach conclusions.

- Theorists like to draw conclusions from the experience by thinking things through logically and objectively.

- Pragmatists plan their next steps by trying out new ideas. They tend to be practical and quick at decision making.

Do any of these sound like someone you know? Or maybe yourself? Do you know your own learning style? If you don't, you can find out by completing the Honey and Mumford questionnaire at www.mint-hr. com/mumford.html.

It's somewhat of a stereotype, but think about a scientist poring over a theory versus a mechanic learning by taking an engine apart, and then putting it all back together. I see these styles in action a lot in training sessions. The people who are done with talking about something and just want to get on and try it for themselves are activists. The people who tend to be quiet, listening to discussions, and then come back with questions at a later time or ask the facilitator something in private are reflectors. The people who aren't satisfied with understanding something at a fairly superficial level and want to know about it in more depth are theorists. And the people who just get on with things are pragmatists.

If you think back to the example of the child playing in the snow, an activist would slide about and fall over a few times; a reflector would watch the activist and learn from their experience before trying it for themselves; a theorist would work out why some areas of snow are more slippery than others; and a pragmatist might test out a few patches, then give it a go.

Some people have put forward the view that rather than learning styles, these are actually personality traits. For example, an activist is someone who will find it hard to sit still at meetings; a reflector is someone who might be quiet in group discussions; a theorist will enjoy detailed, in-depth conversations; and a pragmatist will go with the flow. Either way, these styles or traits influence how a person learns.

The link between personality and learning is an interesting one that has been explored further by Howard Gardner.

Gardner's multiple intelligences

Gardner's multiple intelligences theory[6] applies to personality and behaviour in a work and educational setting as much as it applies to learning styles. He is firmly of the view that people possess a set of intelligences.

---

6   H Gardner, *Frames of Mind: Theory of multiple intelligences* (Fontana Press, 1983)

Think about the person who is gifted mathematically, but finds it difficult to talk to people. Or the person who struggles with maths and languages, but might excel at sports or art. These are examples of the different intelligences in action.

Gardner's seven intelligences are:

- Linguistic: words and language

- Logical-mathematical: numbers

- Musical: sound and rhythm

- Bodily-kinaesthetic: movement control

- Spatial-visual: images and space

- Interpersonal: other people's feelings

- Intrapersonal: self-awareness

Gardner's theory is based on how we perceive and become aware of things. The intelligences indicate not just where people's strengths lie, but also how they prefer to learn. For example, a person who is strong musically and weak numerically might be more likely to develop numerical skills through music. Perhaps singing the times tables might help?

The more you play to a person's strengths when helping them to learn, the more enjoyable the learning process will be and the more effective the training. Whether you subscribe to the specifics of Gardner's theory or not, it highlights that people learn differently and are stimulated by different things and approaches. Variety is the key; this is something that we use to make Taye Training sessions engaging for everyone.

The VAK model

This is the last theory I'm going to look at. The VAK model is:[7]

- Visual: seeing and reading. Learning by watching demonstrations, looking at diagrams, pictures, etc.

- Auditory: listening and speaking. Learning by listening to others speak, by asking questions and by listening to sounds.

- Kinaesthetic: touching and doing. Learning by touching, holding, practical sessions.

These represent preferences or dominant styles, but some people will have an even mix of all three VAK styles or a preference for two of them.

If we think back once again to the example of playing in the snow, most people will use a mix of all three styles. We might want someone to tell us which

7   W B Barbe, M Milone, R H Swassing, *Teaching Through Modality Strength: Concepts and practices* (Zaner-Bloser, 1979)

areas of snow are the most slippery; we might want someone else to show us how to slide safely; we might want to test it out for ourselves; or we might prefer a combination of two or all of those options. In training, it's the role of the facilitator to bring everything together, and ensure that people are motivated and believe they can learn.

Some learning has to be a mix. If you are studying to be a doctor, most people would be a bit alarmed if you learned only by watching someone else, without completing a course of study. But equally, they would be alarmed if you said you had learned how to perform a complex surgical procedure by reading a textbook.

The VAK model is important when you're considering how to design a training session. If someone has a preferred kinaesthetic style and the session involves no practical work, they may become bored and disengaged, so mix up theory with demonstrations and practical sessions to provide something for everyone. Also, as with the doctor example, some things must be learned using a mix of the styles. It's important for delegates to know not just how to do something in theory, but why they do it and how to do it in practice. That's what I embody through Taye Training sessions, and what I advise you to embody in your training for the best outcomes.

Practical application of the learning styles

How do you now put all this theory into practice? First of all, I wouldn't advise you to sit down to plan a session by thinking, 'I must make sure I take all the seven intelligences into account'. Or, 'How would someone with a diverging style react to this?' It doesn't need to be so complicated or rigid.

An awareness of the different styles – whatever you want to call those styles or believe them to be – always needs to be in your mind, but what you really want to be thinking is 'How can I make this learning engaging, so that it's as easy as possible for people to retain essential knowledge and they are motivated to do so?' There are enough common themes in the theories to enable you to know that sessions have to be a mix of practical versus theory, versus time for reflection, to play to people's strengths and preferred ways of learning. Add to that the principles of accelerated learning (which we'll cover later in this chapter) and an experienced facilitator leading the training, and it's a magical mix.

Discussions and activities take account of learning styles/personalities, too. Some people won't like to do a lot of reading or listening. Some won't want to be thrown in at the deep end without notes and instructions. Some will quickly become bored if they don't get the chance for some hands-on experience.

Some won't be comfortable answering questions until they've had a chance to ponder and reflect.

The world is full of all shapes and sizes, and all sorts of different personalities. That's what makes us unique and interesting, so you want your training to be unique and interesting too. It's all about mixing things up to recognise the differences in people and to meet everyone's needs.

We talked about facilitators earlier in this book. They play a critical role in making sessions engaging and interactive, bringing a strong mix of sector knowledge and experience, an ability to expertly apply accelerated learning techniques and principles, and an ability to switch easily between training methods to appeal to different styles and help people who might not immediately grasp something. This is Training 4 Influence in action.

The more experiences you give people, and the more you can help them to reflect and draw conclusions from those experiences, the more easily the learning you deliver will be validated and used to develop further learning. It can also motivate people to learn more on a broader range of subjects. I love it when I see a spark for learning being ignited on one of my courses. It makes my job so worthwhile.

Accelerated learning

The second ingredient that makes training courses engaging and interactive is accelerated learning, which is a concept I absolutely love. I'm going to give you a bit of background about accelerated learning, so that you have some context before we get into how to use it when you're delivering training.

The theory and practical application of accelerated learning is derived from work by many psychologists and education professionals into areas such as the brain, multiple intelligences and learning styles. Thankfully, Colin Rose came along and took all of their work and distilled it down into a simple model of learning that works and makes effective learning available to everyone.[8]

Colin Rose is credited with developing many of the accelerated learning techniques that are used today. He was responsible for pioneering the method with students, teachers and those learning languages.

As the name suggests, accelerated learning allows delegates to learn more in less time and with less effort. It means:

- Creating a positive and enjoyable learning environment

---

8   B Tracy, C Rose, *Accelerated Learning Techniques: The express track to super intelligence* (Simon & Schuster, 1996)

- Working with the whole person – emotional, mental and physical – by delivering information in an engaging way

- Encouraging collaboration between delegates

- Encouraging delegates to help develop their own knowledge

- Allowing delegates to practise and use their new knowledge

If you're thinking 'That doesn't sound like rocket science', you're correct. It's actually relatively easy to incorporate accelerated learning into training, once you know what you're doing, and it makes for a much better experience for everyone.

What's even better, accelerated learning has a big impact on delegates' ability to learn *and* improves retention of knowledge rates because of its multi-dimensional nature. It improves their ability to problem solve and it's been estimated to cut classroom time down by up to 50%. That's pretty impressive.

When you relate this back to the present state of the criminal justice, social care and charity sectors – lack of funding, pressure on services, the need to get better value for money – you can, I'm sure, see why accelerated learning is such a great tool. Not only does it mean that people learn more quickly and effectively so you can deliver more content for the organisation's time and money, but the added bonuses of increased knowledge retention and problem-solving skills mean that delegates will deliver more efficiently when they're back in the office.

What is accelerated learning?

Accelerated learning is a process that engages all of your senses – sight, hearing, smell, touch, taste – to help you retain information more easily. Based on research that suggests people learn best when they have a variety of options allowing them to use all their senses, it works by engaging different parts of the brain during training, making it a more natural process. For example, someone might be listening to something, but at the same time engaging another one or more of their other senses.

Accelerated learning follows the principle that learners don't absorb knowledge, they create it. I love this concept. It is activity-based rather than presentation-based. That's not to say that you won't use presentations at all in your training, but you'll most definitely avoid the dreaded death by PowerPoint. The idea is that delegates submerge themselves in the learning process and, as a result, are able to absorb many things at once.

Think about how babies and young children learn. They pick things up, touch them, move parts about, put toys in their mouths, bring them up to their noses and shake them to see what noise they make. A child often learns how the different parts of a toy work before its parents do. That's because children learn instinctively and naturally, whereas as adults, we often lose or forget this ability, falling into learning by rote and other more traditional methods.

As we develop through the education system, we can also lose or forget our ability to be creative. I wonder whether it's actually more the case that moving away from instinctive learning quashes our creative abilities. These abilities are still present, though, as is our ability to learn and store memories through our senses.

Traditional education directs us how to learn. Young children choose how to learn, and they usually do it through play and creativity, using their imagination and all of their senses without necessarily being consciously aware. And they have fun while they do it. We all learn best when we choose how to learn, and the learning appeals to all of our senses. That's what you want to aim to do during your training sessions – engage all of your delegates' brains and senses so that learning is more instinctive, natural and fun.

Think about a class or course you have attended where you felt the training moved too slowly, was too dry or involved too much sitting about listening to the trainer. How quickly did you become bored? Did you find yourself yawning, looking at your watch, perhaps even having to consciously force yourself to stay awake? In that scenario, did you find it difficult to learn? To retain the knowledge? Did you switch off and miss some of what the trainer was saying? If the whole course was like this, how much do you think you learned? That's the kind of training I so fervently want you to avoid, which is why I fully embrace the use of accelerated learning techniques.

Now consider the converse of that scenario. The facilitator delivers the training in a way that stimulates your senses, so that you are encouraged to connect with and create your own learning, have fun and learn instinctively. Doesn't that sound like a better option? How much do you think you would learn in this situation? And as a trainer, wouldn't you rather have your delegates coming away from your sessions buzzing and re-motivated, rather than bored and demotivated?

The benefits to accelerated learning are massive. Delegates will:

- Be motivated to learn more

- Retain information for longer

- Retain more information in a shorter time

- Continue learning after the course

These are great learner outcomes. And the organisations you work with will benefit too, through more engaged staff, better use of training budgets, better service delivery, more effective teams, and a sense from employees that the organisation cares enough about them to invest so wisely in their development. It's a win-win.

What does accelerated learning mean in practice?

It simply means delivering training in a way that appeals to people's senses, stimulating their desire for learning. They get into a mindset of wanting to learn rather than learning because someone said they had to attend the training course. Then they learn without being consciously aware of everything they are taking in.

Accelerated learning in practice is about creating an environment where people are drawing the learning from you and each other rather than you imparting your experience to them. That can be quite a subtle shift, but so powerful.

The first thing to do is encourage delegates to involve their senses. This might mean:

- Eating while they learn. At Taye Training sessions, we always have sweets and fruit on the table.

- Touching different fabrics or toys – we have a selection of stress toys and gadgets for people to use while the facilitators are talking.

- Drawing or colouring in to engage the delegates' conscious mind, which opens up the unconscious mind to absorb more information. It's also a great stress buster.

- Having music playing.

- Learning by smell (eg making different scented pens available).

Can you think back to a favourite teacher at school or university who was really good at explaining things in a different way if you were struggling to understand? Someone who gave you a practical demonstration or application to help illustrate a point. Someone whose class you always enjoyed. Their classes made you feel motivated to learn and there was always lots of discussion and a buzz. That was accelerated learning in action. You probably remember more of what that teacher taught you than you do from the classes where you were expected to learn in one way or to speak only when spoken to.

Accelerated learning practices on their own bring all sorts of benefits to the learning experience. But when you combine them with an experienced facilitator who not only knows how to use accelerated learning to best effect, but is also a subject matter expert, the results are fantastic. All our facilitators at Taye Training are experienced in their own subject area *and* in accelerated learning techniques.

It's no secret that some of us learn best by doing. If the subject to be learned involves physical skills, such as using equipment, then I find the most effective way of learning can be to get up and move about, practising those skills. We lock knowledge in through repeated muscle movement so that it becomes an unconscious skill.

Think about learning to drive. We start off being aware of everything we're doing – every gear change, touch of the pedals, how the windscreen wipers and indicators work, the route we're taking, the road signs and everything associated with driving. We practise and practise until we get to a point where these things become second nature. We no longer need to consciously think about them because they're locked into our unconscious.

Here is a case example that demonstrates the positive impact of learning styles and accelerated learning.

CASE EXAMPLE

Taye Training was delivering a professional boundaries session for a charity that works with young people convicted of offences. The delegates consisted of volunteers, operational staff, middle management and senior management.

The session was tailored to the organisational needs, so we knew it was completely relevant to the customer group, but we were told that some of the attendees may struggle to sit for the duration of the session as they hadn't ever attended formal education. When I explained that all our courses cater for all learning styles, I could hear trepidation in the 'OK' in response.

If you are familiar with professional boundaries training, you'll know that it's an extremely emotive subject, and delegates can react strongly to different aspects, based on their own personal or professional experience. It can be hard for them to process the sheer amount of information, particularly if it is just presented as slide after slide.

The session had items to stimulate all senses on the table and was broken into half-hour slots, changing the learning style for each element. We would spend five minutes on essential slides before moving on to different activities.

For example:

- We used a signs and symptoms exercise, which was a race against the clock to complete the flipcharts stuck all around the room, followed by a full group discussion.
- The explanation of domestic abuse was a video, followed by a 'What would you do?' task list.
- The values and principle exercise involved people standing up if they agreed with a particular statement or sitting down if they didn't.

In addition to lunch, we had a morning and afternoon break, with music playing and card games for relaxation. At the end, the organiser and some delegates waited behind to thank us. Their concerns had all been addressed as we'd kept them engaged throughout the day.

People often groan when we tell them how interactive our sessions are, yet the feedback is always phenomenal. We work hard so that every delegate has their personal learning needs met. If they are giving us a day of their time, we want to make sure it is worthwhile for them by making the case examples, activities and learning relevant to their daily concerns and customer group, and using engaging learning methods.

The learning process

Even though we all have different learning styles and we seek to learn in our preferred ways, the process we go through tends to be the same. It's the way that Kolb described it: we have an experience; we reflect on it; we draw theories or conclusions about it; we put these theories or conclusions to the test, so we can validate what we've learned and apply the learning to other situations.

Think of the child who touches a hot plate and feels pain. They reflect and reach the conclusion that it was touching the hot plate that caused the pain. This leads them to resolve not to touch the plate again. That's the learning process. Over time, they put that learning to the test and discover that not all plates are hot. They will also learn ways to tell which plates are hot and which aren't, so they continue to use the process to expand their learning.

People might have to experience something several times to work out what the learning is. That could be because there are several variables: why does the car keep breaking down? Is it a lack of petrol, a mechanical or electrical failure, lack of maintenance etc? Or it could be that their brains are slow to absorb certain pieces of information because of how the information is presented to them. Maybe they don't understand a maths equation the first time they're shown it. Or it might be because their brains don't want to be believe what they're seeing. This can be especially true of optical illusions, but it also applies in other areas of life. As a result, people repeat the same process and test out their theories and conclusions, until eventually they learn why something is happening.

Sometimes we seek out the learning because we *want* to – we want to know how to ride a bike to have fun with our friends. Sometimes we seek out the learning because we *have* to – we have to learn about legislative changes which impact on our roles. Sometimes learning is *imposed* on us – our employer might recommend that we go through refresher training as part of a performance management process or because of an inspection.

Some of us might like to take notes or read books and underline sections. Some might want to learn by repetition or go over practical demonstrations several times. Some people are constantly hungry for knowledge and learn in a variety of ways. Some people are fast learners, others learn more slowly, but once they gain the knowledge, they retain it for a long time. Some people will become knowledgeable in a lot of areas; others will become experts in one. Some people only want to learn to a certain point, and then no more.

The internal process is pretty much always the same, even if someone isn't a willing participant in the training. If they're learning something they will seldom need to use, people may have to refer back to training materials to remind them of what they've learned. But if it's something they are going to use repeatedly, it will become a habit and pass from the unconscious to the conscious mind, and back to the unconscious – from unconscious incompetence to unconscious competence.[9] That's when the learning has become fully embedded.

Let's take learning to drive as an example again:

- Unconscious incompetence – when we first start, we don't know what we don't know.

- Conscious incompetence – as we practise, we know what we need to learn to pass our test, but we haven't learned it yet.

---

9   The model was first described by Martin M Broadwell in 1969 in *The Gospel Guardian* but similar models were used by other authors subsequently.

- Conscious competence – we have to think about it, but we know how to change gear, reverse, parallel park, do three-point turns, etc.

- Unconscious competence – we are able to operate a lot of the processes in the car without thinking. When we describe ourselves as having driven somewhere on automatic pilot, that's unconscious competence at play.

I'm sure you've heard that when people have been in a life-or-death situation, they have reported the phenomenon of seeing their whole life flashing in front of their eyes. That's actually the brain frantically searching through its memory banks to examine every experience the person has ever had and all the learning they've accumulated to find a solution to their perilous predicament. Unconscious competence is fascinating stuff, and it ably demonstrates the power of using processes and techniques, such as accelerated learning and taking account of different styles, to firmly embed the learning in delegates' unconscious minds. Taking account of learning styles helps to speed up the process of moving through the phases of competence, makes learning more engaging for different people, makes it more effective and increases retention rates.

As you go through the Training 4 Influence methodology, each point will connect together. Although each step is important in its own right, together they are game changers. Interactive and engaging training sounds like a simple concept. Often when I talk to trainers, they tell me their sessions are interactive and engaging, they consider learning styles, etc. When I speak to delegates, they can sometimes see things differently.

CASE EXAMPLE

I recently assessed an organisation against the Training 4 Influence standards. The trainers the organisation was using were delivering a course which was accredited and recommended by government agencies. The information was excellent, detailed and current. The trainers were operational experts and tailored the learning to the organisation, so they were really surprised when we fed back that they hadn't met the interactive and engaging standard.

Although the trainers absolutely did use activities in the session, they didn't use them often enough and the activities didn't differ significantly enough from each other. Big chunks of time were dedicated to PowerPoint presentations, and for part of the session, delegates didn't move for nearly two hours.

This doesn't mean that the course wasn't good; it was fantastic. But it did mean that not every delegate had the same opportunity to learn, and none of the delegates met their potential for understanding and retaining information.

When we assess, we assess across all learning styles. We have a checklist of every style we want to cover and consider these when writing the session. No matter how interactive and engaging your sessions are, I recommend you take a look at your audience. Are they *all* fully engaged *all* of the time? Possibly not.

You can download examples of different activities we use at Taye to cover the learning styles and a checklist to help you ensure you have activities that meet different needs at https://training4influence.co.uk/resources/

CHAPTER TOP TIPS

How to make your training sessions engaging:

- An easy win is to add fiddle toys, sweets and colouring resources to the tables. You'll be surprised at the difference this makes.
- Start the session with some emotional learning. It connects people to the subject and keeps them engaged for longer.
- Get people moving to stimulate their brains and get the oxygen flowing. Include at least two or three activities where they need to move around.
- Change the delivery style every twenty to thirty minutes ie using PowerPoint/verbal activity/ movement activity/written activity etc.
- Add music to play over lunch and breaks to aid relaxation.
- Use talking instead of listening by asking learners to explain learning points to each other and/or the full group.

- Include an optional workbook or printout of the slides. Some delegates like to write to increase absorption and retention of knowledge.

- Watch a video clip together and ask delegates to give a summary on the key points.

- Be mindful of the temperature, location and facilities. A warm, dark room makes people feel sleepy.

- Ask a delegate to teach someone else what they are learning. If a delegate knows that they are responsible for teaching someone else, they will pay more attention to the material.

5
Values

Earlier in the book, we discussed why the approach of the facilitator, the perspectives they share with the delegates, and each and every training session they deliver all have the ability to influence. We reflected on how Training 4 Influence is a creative solution to make the most out of ordinary training sessions, whatever the subject.

Now we have reached the final element of the methodology, you will have seen glimpses of this already throughout the book. If you truly deliver values-based training, your why runs like a golden thread throughout the entire session, influencing all your responses and activities.

This chapter is slightly different to the others. That's because I can't teach you a technique for being values-based; as a facilitator, you need to feel this, recognising the power of treating people well and delivering exceptional services. The aim of this chapter is to help you realise the importance of bringing your values-based perspective to life in your courses.

When we analysed Taye courses to find out why we received such fantastic feedback, we never realised values would feature as one of the top reasons. It wasn't something we had recruited for. It just so happened that because we'd recruited people like us – people who really care about individuals – Faye and I had ensured that the facilitators would come with similar values to ours. It was years later that we realised this is the magical aspect of our method.

In this chapter, we'll look at the values we hold, valuing ourselves and valuing others plus values-based decision making. We give examples from our experience delivering training to frontline professionals who are working with complex and/or vulnerable people, but the lessons and influence are the same across all sectors, in all training. People are people.

Why values are so important

You can be an operational expert, an accomplished trainer and have developed a tailored session which considers all learning styles, but if you don't deliver the content from a values-based perspective, the transformation that you, the organisations you work with and the delegates who attend your sessions are all looking for simply won't happen.

Let's delve a bit deeper into the subject of values. It's a word we often hear bandied about, but what does it actually mean? What are values?

You might find different definitions, but my own is the one that resonates most with me:

Values are the important beliefs and needs you hold that influence all areas of life.

We all find it easy and comfortable to make decisions and take actions that align with our values. If we make decisions that conflict with our values, this can cause discomfort and dissatisfaction. This discomfort and dissatisfaction has a name: cognitive dissonance.[10]

Cognitive dissonance arises when our behaviour or attitude is at odds with our values. It makes us feel guilty, uncomfortable, ashamed, anxious, embarrassed, angry with ourselves and, if it's extreme, worthless and full of self-loathing. For example, this is what happens to the gambler who has promised their family that they won't gamble anymore, and then

---

10   L Festinger, *A Theory of Cognitive Dissonance* (Stanford University Press, 1957)

finds themselves betting on horses. They value their family and their integrity, but have behaved at odds with these values.

The best way to reduce the negative feelings associated with cognitive dissonance is to change the behaviour. But we, as human beings, can be stubborn creatures and often we try to avoid the feeling of dissonance in irrational ways, such as justifying our behaviours. In our example of the gambler, they may justify their behaviour by telling themselves that they were trying to win money to better provide for their family.

The opposite of cognitive dissonance is cognitive consonance, when we act entirely in keeping with our values, and this gives rise to feelings of internal harmony and happiness. Those are the feelings you want to help create on your courses.

Talk of values has become really popular lately. If we are living aligned with our values, we will be happier, healthier and more fulfilled humans, and this recognition has been transformational for many. I love this and completely agree. My values are intrinsically linked to everything I do. They are arguably the reason I have written this book.

I wonder if you'll think I am going too far if I say that values are the be all and end all? Hopefully not. Are you nodding along?

At the start of the book, I told you a little of my story. I shared how I was compelled to work in this field – compelled to recognise the power frontline professionals have and help them deliver life-changing services. All of that is true, but the key to it happening is recognising someone's worth; recognising that people, just by being human, have equal value in society.

Our opinion of people should never be based on possessions, status, behaviour; these are all irrelevant. Holding on to the right values and delivering services aligned to them is absolutely key, and Training 4 Influence helps frontline professionals in this way. It helps them to recognise that, when they're working with people who have complex needs and/or are vulnerable, they need to consider values from a multi-dimensional perspective, because the outcome of their work can be life limiting or life improving.

If, like me, you've worked in criminal justice, social care or a charity for a while, I hope you already subscribe to the concept that people change people. For that to happen, human connection and opportunity are key. These are then affirmed by environment.

I delivered a TEDx talk, explaining how and why I believe connection, opportunity and environment, when they're working together, are life-changing. On their own, they make a difference, but collectively, they have the power to help someone transform their life – when the individual is ready.

Frontline professionals hold the key to connection, opportunity and environment, but only if they are delivering services from a values-based perspective. Values are their back-up, their safety net, their go to. They should lead decision making and help professionals feel aligned with the work they do.

Let's have a look at the tools and techniques to encourage and support change while championing a values-based approach to service delivery.

Your values

Have you ever thought about your values? Some of you will have and some won't. There is no right answer. Often, we're not consciously aware of our values until we're asked to do something that is at odds with them. Then we become aware of them via our internal discomfort.

When I thought about my values, it was enlightening to label them. I say 'label' because that's what I was doing. They weren't new; I've always had values, some steady and consistent, some have changed multiple times over the years. But for me, they were never previously named.

If you check out the Taye Training website or my LinkedIn profile, you'll see I proudly state my values as:

- Integrity

- Fairness

- Honesty

- Safety

- Commitment

These matter to me. In some guise or another, they always have and probably always will, but how I interpret their meaning has changed. You may be reading them and inferring a completely different meaning to me. That's OK; it's normal because of your current frame of reference, which is something we'll talk a little more about when we get to values-based decision making. But for now, let's focus on our individual values. If you haven't thought specifically about your values you can download a worksheet to help you explore your values at https://training4influence. co.uk/resources/

If you are an operational expert, someone who works, has previously worked or has personal experience in the criminal justice and/or social care sectors, then the chances are you were drawn to the work or the training because of your values. Just like the delegates will have been. You recognise that frontline professionals absolutely have the power to change lives and you want to be part of making that difference. The big questions here is why? Why didn't you or haven't you chosen to go stack shelves in a supermarket instead? People tell me it's a lot less stressful.

A person's why is intrinsically connected to their values, and both are born from life experiences. I'll use my story as an example. My why was born in my own childhood, but realised due to my education and opportunity. I've always wanted to prevent others suffering in a similar way to me, and my professional experience has given me the knowledge and tools to realise it is possible.

We *can* stop the generational cycle of harm and abuse. Because of my experiences, I am naturally drawn to working with young people, homelessness, substance misuse, people who have been convicted of offences and those the system has made powerless to make change. I seek out the most complex of situations and try to influence them because I truly believe we all have to make the change we want to see.

Not everybody's why is quite so extreme, but you may be surprised by how many are. Either directly or indirectly, people may have experienced, witnessed or perpetrated harm, and their why for working in frontline services is driven by a real emotional connection. There is a debate about the right time to work in a service if you are driven by emotions, but this is not the time for it.

Lived experience is a popular term at the moment. And without a doubt, there are immense benefits for people who have lived experience to come to work in services, but it has to be at the right time for them, and they might not always be the best judge of that. I'm twenty+ years past my trauma, but I'm still triggered and still need to recognise my limitations.

Your why will be connected to your experience, your life journey, something you have learned along the way. I asked some of Taye's facilitators why they deliver training and got some great answers. They talked about 'helping people realise what they're capable of', 'giving back to a sector that changed their life' and 'empowering people to deliver life-changing services'. At the beginning of every single training session, we ask the delegates for their why. We help them uncover – or rediscover – and explore their why for doing what they do so that we can then use that knowledge where needed to reignite their passion.

People working in social care, charity and criminal justice often enter the field with a strong ideology. They want to help change lives, solve complex societal issues and make a difference. But systems, recurring legislative and policy changes, reduced funding and increasing caseloads distract them from what was once their most important reason for undertaking the role. Reminding them of the granular detail, the lives they are changing and the difference they are making every day is so important because, as frontline professionals, they can often get overwhelmed with frustration at the things they can't change. In every Taye session we ask delegates their 'why' at the beginning and connect the learning to their answers as we go through the session. You can download an example 'why' activity at https://training4influence. co.uk/resources/

When you're a facilitator, there really is nothing better at the end of a training session than having a delegate thank you for reminding them of why they love their job. They might recount their why slowly and without emotion at the beginning of the day, but by the end, when they have connected it to the change, impact and fulfilment they've experienced throughout the session, their eyes come back to life and it is magical to watch. Every single person working in criminal justice, social care or charities – and, actually, society at large – has the power to change lives, prevent abuse and increase opportunities for those who are marginalised and vulnerable.

The organisation's why

Another important aspect of the facilitator's role is to help the delegates recognise the synergy between their own personal why and their organisation's why, and that's what we'll look at next.

We spoke briefly in the 'Tailored' chapter about how important it is to connect a training session clearly to the organisation's mission, vision and values. Let's look at why.

Nowadays, you tend to find that most organisations have a vision, mission and values. For some organisations, these will sit stagnant on the website, while others will have employees who literally live and breathe their values.

People working within complex frontline services often join an organisation because of its vision, mission and values. I certainly did. But vision, values and mission are no good if they are not brought to life. They should direct an organisation's operations and be integrated throughout every single training session or they become meaningless words on a piece of paper, and no one can relate what they do back to the organisation's ethos. Which is truly a shame as that ethos may be exactly why someone joined the organisation in the first place.

At worst, without the organisation linking everything back to the words on a piece of paper, there is a real risk of people developing their own agendas. In the absence of any other guidance, no one is pulling together to deliver the best outcomes. If there are no organisational values, people will use their own personal values to direct their work. And if everyone is doing their own thing, it can lead to a lack of consistency.

That's where Training 4 Influence is a game changer. There are two aspects to why it's critical to know the organisation's mission, vision and values before you create a training proposal and design a course. The first is to connect to them throughout the training session, which helps the organisation to embed its values and make clear to employees what its overall purpose and direction is. This helps to bring the mission, vision and values to life, instead of them just being words written on a piece of paper. And this is important because, when money is tight and staff are under immense pressure, their activity has to be focused on the right things and in the right way to make sure that money is spent effectively and for the benefit of customers.

The second reason is that it will make the training much more effective because the facilitator has a clear picture of what the organisation wants to achieve and the behaviours that are important. For example, if one of the values is built around excellence in service delivery, the facilitator wants to know about that and feed it into every session. They also want to make sure that the delegates all have the same understanding of what excellence in their organisation looks like. And by organisations investing in employees in the most effective way, they ensure their employees feel valued and motivated to stay and work hard.

If the values and vision aren't already embedded throughout the organisation, training will help them to become so. Conversely, if they are embedded and they aren't included in the training, delegates won't engage in the course to the same extent.

If you integrate the mission, values and vision of each organisation into every part of each course you deliver, not only does it make the session specific to the organisation, but it also means the session is much easier for delegates to relate to and their learning will be greater. That gives you, as the facilitator, greater satisfaction and everyone enjoys the training much more. If this sounds like an onerous process, it isn't. It takes minutes to do – less if you're an internal trainer – yet makes such a huge difference.

The benefits of delivering training that incorporates each organisation's mission, vision and values far outweigh the time it takes to connect them. This kind of training increases productivity, as employees will feel connected to the organisation and be more focused on its why. This helps them absorb learning more quickly, making them more effective in their roles. In other words, it increases the effectiveness of training.

When the facilitator incorporates the organisation's why into training, the organisation can benefit almost immediately through increased knowledge and improved skills. Long term, it benefits through changed attitudes, a positive culture and staff retention. Employees can be far more forgiving of disruption, pressure and chaos if they feel connected to the journey the organisation is on.

Ultimately, if you connect the organisation's values, vision and mission to your training sessions, it enables you to deliver training from a values-based perspective. What this means is making sure that the organisational values are woven – with that golden thread I've spoken about – into every aspect of the training. You then deliver learning and teach skills that are aligned with the organisation's values.

CASE EXAMPLE

Let me use Taye's Managing Challenging Behaviour course as an example.

There are many positive and negative ways to manage challenging behaviour. Within our course, we discuss safety, positive de-escalation, recognising an individual's role in crucial conversations and professional responsibility. Connecting this approach to an organisation's mission, vision and values is powerful, as delegates see we are helping them deliver services in line with the organisation's ethos – which is what they signed up for.

As you read the rest of this chapter, think about an organisation you are delivering training for at the moment. How hard would it be to connect the points of your session to the organisation's vision, values and mission? If it's an organisation working to make change – criminal justice, social care or charity – I'd make a bet they'd fit quite naturally. When they're woven throughout the course, they further embed the organisation's personal message to its staff and customers.

Values-based decision making

Values-based decision making is a way of making critical decisions that takes account of the things an individual or organisation values most. Using this approach helps to identify what the crucial decisions are and what information to consider to make those decisions most effectively.

In the courses I deliver, I ask people to imagine that, in life, they have an invisible suitcase that trails along behind them. Every time they have a conversation, read a book (or social media post), go somewhere or undertake an activity, a remnant, sometimes big, sometimes small, jumps into the suitcase. That suitcase becomes their frame of reference, and everything they look at in the future, every decision they make – everything is influenced by what they have in their suitcase. Things can be taken out, but they need to be consciously taken out.

This may sound simplistic, but it gets the point across, particularly as Taye delegates take part in a connected activity to highlight the point. Let me give you an example.

CASE EXAMPLE

Delegates are shown an imaginary line in the training room, with one end standing for very concerned, the opposite end for not concerned at all. I read out a statement and delegates are asked to place themselves along the line depending on their level of concern, based on the statement.

It's interesting to see different people standing in different places, even though they work for the same organisation and have the same information and policies available to them. There are also differences if I do the exercise with one organisation compared to another.

Here is an example of the type of statement I might read out and the variance in responses. 'You are with a man who has a heroin addiction and is in treatment. His wife has left him and he has sole care of their one-year-old daughter.' With some groups, I would find a high level of people who were really concerned about the situation, feeling that it might be wrong for the man to be in charge of his daughter. But groups of substance-misuse workers tend to have much lower levels of concern.

Even where people are doing the same job for the same organisation, there are always different answers. This is because people have different frames of reference: different experiences are influencing their decision making.

I stress that there are no right or wrong answers. I also stress that every time someone makes a decision like this in a professional capacity, it impacts on someone's life, sometimes in a profound way. It's about working together to get to the right outcome, which can be done by speaking to other people to get another perspective.

At Taye, we have a variety of similar activities which we use as required across all of our courses. People tend to assume that other people think and feel like they do, but this isn't always the case. One of our facilitators described this perfectly in our Training 4 Influence podcast. He was discussing the key learning points of Taye's Managing Challenging Behaviour course. He explained how, for young people, he uses the term 'window of your world' as they understand how this means their view is limited.

Doing this activity prompts an intense discussion, which can lead experienced staff to change their minds. It can also have a profound effect on new staff, who can be idealistic and want to have all the answers and to get things right. When they see their more experienced colleagues consider different perspectives and perhaps change their own, it effectively gives them permission to ask for help and realise that it's OK *not* to have the answer to everything themselves. This can have a hugely positive impact on someone's professional and personal development. I find it so rewarding when I see little lightbulbs going on around the room.

More often than not, values-based activities lead on to conversations about unconscious bias. People feel the need to verbalise that 'they are not biased in any way'. Helping people realise that of course they are (think back to the invisible suitcase) is an insightful and game-changing part of training courses.

Unconscious bias is a fascinating subject. Each of us would probably like to believe that we are free from biased, stereotyping and discriminatory thoughts. But the reality is that most, if not all people carry some form of unconscious bias. That's quite a disturbing thought, but we are all human and we all have different life experiences that shape us. The key thing is to become aware of the unconscious biases we have, so we can do something about them, or at least recognise when our biases might be about to influence our decisions.

Our brains are wired to allow us to make quick unconscious decisions. If we had to consciously mull over every option open to us throughout the day before making a decision, we would be overwhelmed. For example, we don't consciously think, 'Should I get dressed before I have my shower or after?' We unconsciously follow a process that we've learned over a long period – in this example, preferring to go out in dry clothes.

That might seem like a bit of a ridiculous example, but it illustrates that we are unconsciously making decisions throughout the day. These unconscious decisions are formed and influenced by our background, upbringing, education, culture and personal experiences. It's the same for our opinions – we hold unconscious views that can impact on decisions we make. This includes us all instinctively and unconsciously categorising people based on age, weight, skin colour, gender, educational level, disability, sexuality, accent, social status and job title. And that's not an exhaustive list...

This can lead us to develop stereotypes and biases without realising we have them. And sometimes, we rely on those stereotypes and biases, even if we don't consciously believe them. According to an article in *The Guardian*,[11] neuroscientists have established that stereotypes begin to form in early childhood and can be fuelled by negative perceptions in the media. We involuntarily absorb information from all around us and, as such, are not aware of all the biases we develop.

Grouping together with people who share our biases helps us to make sense of the world and protects us from information overload. The problem with this approach is that our prejudice becomes hard-wired

---

11 S Boseley, 'Children are straitjacketed into gender roles in early adolescence, says study', *The Guardian*, 2017, www.theguardian.com/society/2017/sep/20/children-are-straitjacketed-into-gender-roles-in-early-adolescence-says-study

into our brains. And unfortunately, these biases can then seep into our decisions and actions without us being aware, affecting outcomes.

Doing an activity which flushes out some unconscious biases can allow individuals, teams and organisations to make big leaps ahead in the quality and fairness of service delivery. As a facilitator, you need to do this in a supportive way so that no one feels exposed, ridiculed or judged.

CASE EXAMPLE

Do you remember the audience's reaction to Susan Boyle when she first walked on to the *Britain's Got Talent* stage? There was unkind laughter directed at her appearance and the way she interacted with the judges. There were hints of a possible learning disability, but this didn't lead to a sympathetic reception. Quite the opposite, as if people felt that someone with a learning disability shouldn't have entered a high-profile competition in front of a live audience and an even larger TV following.

The opening bars of music were heard. It was a song from *Les Misérables*: a big song, needing a fantastic voice to carry it off. Everyone waited with bated breath for what they expected to be car-crash TV.

But then Susan Boyle began to sing and immediately people's perceptions changed. The judges' jaws dropped; the audience let out gasps. Against the odds, against all their preconceived ideas, she could really sing.

Imagine if the crowd had had the power to stop her
from entering the competition, based only on her
appearance and the things she said. How many people
would have allowed her to sing?

That's unconscious bias in action. Susan Boyle's example illustrates how easy it could be to make a decision that is harmful to someone's future. It's a fork-in-the-road moment.

Why is mitigating your biases and pursuing values-based decision making so important? Frontline professionals could 'stop people entering the competition' every day. We make safeguarding decisions, service decisions, engagement decisions... we hold that power. Every single day, we come to a fork-in-the-road moment with someone. Only by recognising and challenging our own unconscious biases can we navigate these forks effectively.

If you place your values at the heart of decision making and bring every decision back to what you value, you are offering the best possible service to the customer. The decision isn't being led by you, it's being explored by everyone around you.

As a facilitator, operating on a values-based perspective is vital to focusing your delegates on the possible and most likely courses of action, based on the particular circumstances presented by the particular service user, in the particular situation. It gives them a framework to work within. It sounds straightforward, but it can be a complicated area.

The aim is to achieve values-based decisions which strike a balance between the complex and conflicting values of those concerned in a given situation. Complex values are those that mean different things to different people, for example, acting with respect. It is important to be clear about what your organisational values really mean and what they look and feel like in practice.

Conflicting values are those that are in conflict with one another, either within an individual or between individuals. They might arise where an individual experiences conflict between their personal and professional values, or where different individuals have different values.

When I talk about values-based decision making, I am talking about making decisions based on the organisational values that will be woven throughout all of the training, recognising that, in any given situation, an individual will naturally bring their own values to bear. For that reason, we, as facilitators, need to focus on building awareness of the diversity of values that exist, awareness of people's individual values and mutual respect for differences of values.

If this sounds like a recipe for chaos, it isn't. It's quite the opposite, actually. When we build this awareness and understanding, it means that delegates can have open discussions about possible courses of action, can listen to and learn from different perspectives, and ultimately make decisions that are values-driven and connect with the objectives of the organisation. This, in turn, gives the customer the best service available.

Valuing others

When we feel truly valued, we can be our best self. This is true in every situation, and so it is true for facilitators, for frontline professionals and for the customers they are working with. In other words, it's true for everyone.

In the professional relationship between frontline worker and customer, the need to be valued is magnified. If we, as frontline workers, want to support someone to change their behaviours or stay safe, we need to treat them well, help them to belong and see that they are connected and part of a community. And, of course, frontline professionals have the power to make decisions that can impact someone's life on a daily basis. We need to make these decisions within the recognition that values influence our decision making.

Many of our behaviours in life are so unconscious and ingrained that we don't stop to think about what we're doing. We're on automatic pilot, doing what we've always done. It's often only when someone encourages us to think differently that we change behaviours.

The best way to change negative behaviours into positive ones is by using positive reinforcement. If you've come across the Good Lives Model,[12] you'll know that it promotes the view that all individuals are naturally goal-seeking, and there are factors that are important in enhancing their motivation and bringing about transformational change. It advocates taking an approach with people which focuses positively on equipping them with the necessary skills to secure what they need, in a socially acceptable way that encourages connection and feelings of belonging, and in a personally meaningful way (ie based around values). If you offer training within the criminal justice and social care sector, bear in mind you may be working with delegates who are vulnerable in some way and need to feel valued and part of the community within their organisation.

A frontline professional can make or break a person's hour, day, life because of the way they respond in the moment. This may seem extreme, but it is true. Let me give you two case examples – I've seen this from both sides.

---

12 For an extensive list of publications, see the Good Lives Model website at www.goodlivesmodel.com/publications.shtml

CASE EXAMPLE

When I was sixteen, my life changed because a frontline professional offered me an opportunity; she gave me hope. But it was more than that – she had the skills to engage with me. She knew who to signpost me to for further support, and I discovered that if she said she was going to do something, she did it, all within her professional capabilities.

This constant doing what she said she was going to do and the boundaries she kept meant I could start to trust adults/services/authorities in a way I never had before. Because of this, over time I embraced human connection and believing in myself. Then, when I was ready, she supported me to change my environment.

If she hadn't been there that day, if she'd been distracted, if she didn't have the skills to engage with me or had been too overwhelmed by her caseload or the system to offer me the first smile, I wouldn't be writing this book today.

CASE EXAMPLE

When I was a supervisor in a homeless hostel, we had a young man living with us who many staff told me was a nightmare. He was angry, abusive and disrespectful. One morning, he threw a stapler at a staff member's head (luckily it missed). The staff asked if they could evict him.

When I asked to meet with him to discuss the stapler incident, he was angry at me too. I told him that his behaviour was unacceptable. He told me to 'f*** off', that the staff member 'deserved it'. He wasn't willing to explain, but equally, I wasn't willing to evict him, as his next stop would be the streets.

I was clear with him that a repeat of his behaviour would result in eviction, and that I wanted us to do everything we could to avoid that. I asked him how we could recognise if he was getting stressed and what to do before he snapped and threw another stapler. He begrudgingly helped me come up with some basic interventions and apologised to the staff member.

Over the next few weeks, I watched the interactions between the staff and this young man. A core group had decided he was trouble, was never going to amount to anything, and was just another waster coming through the hostel system. These weren't their words, but this was what their actions said to me.

When he came into the office, they all looked down. When he asked, 'Has the post been?' he was told to leave the office, knock on the door before entering again and say please. When he opened a letter saying he had an appointment the next week and was visibly upset, he was ignored. In this context, it doesn't surprise me that he threw a stapler. His perception was that all the staff hated him and thought he was worthless.

You'll likely be pleased to know, I stepped in. After some quite intense coaching, the staff members presented differently to the young people in the hostel. It was too late for this lad, though, as he had moved on by this point. I have to hope that he was valued in his next placement.

Frontline professionals don't have to be perfect; we are human, after all. But if we are delivering services from the perspective that everyone we are working with is of equal importance, we won't go far wrong. Role modelling decent human behaviour, acting in line with the values and mission of the organisation we are working with makes *the* difference.

Because all Taye's courses are delivered with values entwined through them, the activities are presented from that perspective. The foundation is the course-specific activity I described earlier that highlights every delegate's frame of reference and bias. This is embedded by every activity being informed by valuing the individual, always within the context of the role. A simple question 'Would you prefer a morning or afternoon appointment?' can make all the difference to someone who has limited power or choices in their usual life.

Trauma informed

In Taye's sessions, we advocate that frontline services have an understanding of the principles of being trauma informed.[13] It's a sad statistic that over 80% of people engaging in frontline services have experienced trauma – some kind of deeply upsetting or disturbing event or series of events producing an overwhelming amount of stress which exceeds their

---

13 M Withers, 'Trauma-informed care and why it matters', *Psychology Today*, 2017, www.psychologytoday.com/gb/blog/modern-day-slavery/201707/trauma-informed-care-and-why-it-matters

ability to cope or integrate the emotions involved. It covers a broad umbrella of things.

When I talk here about services being trauma informed, I don't mean everyone has to be experts in trauma. There are specialist services for people who need that level of intervention. What I mean is having an understanding of the overarching principles, which is so powerful. A lot of vulnerable people who use criminal justice and social care services have experienced trauma. It is more prevalent than you may imagine, and not just among people who are using the services frontline professionals work with.

Not everyone who has experienced trauma will manifest it to the extent that they require the use of these services at the time. It can be a latent issue which may manifest at a much later date, even when the traumatic event has been all but forgotten by everyone who knew about it, with the exception of the person who experienced it. That's why frontline professionals need to be aware of the signs and effects of trauma when they're dealing with a wide range of people. They never know who is going to walk through the door or exactly what life experiences they'll bring with them. If frontline staff don't have the necessary skills to recognise the signs of trauma and deal with it appropriately, this can give rise to challenging behaviour, the risk of someone being re-traumatised and/or not taking up the support that's available to them, perpetuating the cycle of harm, abuse, homelessness, etc.

Trauma isn't just prevalent in the people who use criminal justice, social care and charity services; it can be found in people who work in the public sector too (police, ambulance service, firefighters, mental-health professionals, etc) and in other sectors, such as healthcare and the military. It can be found in any walk of life because we never know what life experiences someone has had. Even if you work as a trainer in an industry where you wouldn't necessarily expect trauma to be prevalent, it doesn't mean you won't encounter people who have lived through it. That's why it's so important that we, as facilitators, inform our delegates about trauma, to make sure they have the skills to recognise the signs and work appropriately with those who have experienced it.

What is trauma?

Trauma can mean different things to different people. They might have experienced it at the hands of one or more people they didn't know. They might have experienced trauma at the hands of a partner, family member or someone who was known to them in a different capacity. They might have experienced trauma as a member of a particular culture or community. Think back to 9/11 and the impact the events of that day would have had on people whose family members were caught up in it, those who were first responders, who witnessed the events on the ground and who saw them on TV.

Trauma can be experienced through adverse child-hood, adulthood, and community and cultural experiences. It can be experienced directly or indirectly. For example, someone might experience trauma by witnessing an abusive relationship as a child.

The impact of trauma can be widespread and have devastating consequences for those affected and their families. Its effects can be long term and last from one generation to the next. Trauma can have many layers to it, and it can be cumulative, ie one event on its own may not trigger a traumatic response, but witnessing or experiencing a number of events over a sustained period can be traumatising.

Trauma impacts on people's emotions, beliefs, values, attitudes, behaviours, relationships, and physical and mental wellbeing. It can cause extreme anxiety and depression, rob people of their trust and security, and restrict the activities that the person will engage in or the places they will go to.

People who have experienced trauma are vulnerable and often marginalised. Experience of trauma can be a risk factor which can lead to physical, social, behavioural and mental-health difficulties. It can lead to people experiencing addictions, homelessness, relationship breakdowns, disabilities, educational issues, sexual health issues and, of course, offending. It can also exacerbate any of these issues, leading to a cycle of harm. Trauma can lead to people having to function in various survival modes, affecting integration and reintegration.

It is important that we, as frontline workers, provide services which are inclusive, realise the need is there for these services, can recognise the signs of trauma and actively respond to reduce its impacts. As we do so, it is important that the services we deliver do not create an experience which causes re-traumatisation or induces further trauma. Nor should they mirror survival modes.

This is about more than raising awareness; it's about creating organisational cultures which promote security, safety and trust. To do this, as facilitators, we need to ensure everyone in an organisation models the type of service and behaviour we want to see. Organisational leaders must realise the widespread and debilitating impact of trauma, recognise its signs and symptoms, understand how to help someone on their journey to recovery, develop practices and policies that support work to reduce the effects of trauma, and actively work against re-traumatisation. And they must do this for customers *and* staff.

This means having a framework to use in relation to trauma, underpinned by the mission, vision, values, principles and practices of the organisation, and constantly learning from feedback, so that the organisation can keep evolving to deliver best practice at all times. Organisational leaders need to make services

TRANSFORM YOUR TRAINING

human and put the person at the centre of everything, which means looking at the organisation's policies, approach to customer engagement and a host of other things, making the organisation a safe haven for the people using the service.

At a practical level, this is about how people are treated the minute they walk through the door and right the way through their use of the service. It's about how they are greeted, how they are spoken to more generally, how they are supported, the signage the organisation uses, the physical environment and so on. It is also important to make sure that staff are trained and supported. Staff wellbeing is at the heart of this – the better they're trained, the healthier and more trauma-informed staff are, the better able they are to support their customers.

There is another important aspect to this. Bearing in mind that the incidence of trauma is higher than many would believe, it is highly likely that some staff members have already experienced trauma them-selves. This may even be a factor that influenced their choice of profession, ie a desire to help others who have experienced similar trauma. Even if the staff have not themselves experienced trauma outside of work, the fact that they are dealing with people who have done so means that they may have experienced trauma and extreme stress at or as a result of their work. This trauma can come from hearing about oth-ers' traumatic experiences, experiencing the death of service users, facing job threats and funding cuts, working in a fractured team, dealing with complaints, making decisions which conflict with their values, dealing with challenging behaviours, being subjected to physical and verbal abuse, and being under ongoing scrutiny and inspection.

At a practical level, we, as facilitators, need to understand the physical, social and emotional impact of trauma on not just the victims, but also the professionals who work with them. We need to understand that this can impact on how vulnerable and marginalised people engage with – or choose not to engage with – service providers and the criminal justice process. We must recognise that policies, processes and services need to ensure that people are not re-traumatised; that they are made to feel safe and that services are delivered effectively.

At Taye, we advocate taking a trauma-informed approach with everyone. This is so that services can support people who have experienced trauma, without having to take steps to identify if every customer has experienced trauma. That could result in labelling and feelings of exclusion.

We use an approach that incorporates the principles of:

- Safety
- Security

- Trustworthiness

- Choice

- Collaboration

- Empowerment

At a practical level, this might mean letting the customer choose the best place and time to meet, letting them choose the type of room and whether they see a male or female member of staff.

If an organisation doesn't take this kind of approach, vulnerable people will either choose not to engage with its services, or will engage but find the process ineffective at best and traumatic at worst. And above all, it will do nothing to build trust, so that vulnerable people may never engage or re-engage with the services, with potentially devastating consequences. The cycle continues and the risk of harm or death for the vulnerable person increases.

Valuing ourselves

'You can't give anyone a lift if your tank is empty.'
— Faye Fox

When you get on an aeroplane, one of the first things you are told is in the event of an emergency, please put on your own air mask before you help someone put on theirs. This perfectly illustrates one of the basics of professional emotional resilience. Keep your own oxygen supply topped up first, so you have enough to share.

The Training 4 Influence methodology was developed specifically because the sector I love so much is in crisis – the sector with so much potential. Much of this crisis, unfortunately, is being borne personally by frontline professionals. Good people are burning out, trying so hard in a complex, ever-changing system; a system that asks for more for less and expects change to be fast and long-standing.

I know so many amazing people (many of whom are now trainers) who have left the criminal justice, charity and social care sectors because of the impact the role was having on their health and families. Sleepless nights, no time with loved ones, mental-health problems – the list goes on and on. In a sector that recognises that people change people, this is a poor show. It is expecting professionals to give everything, to perform, to change lives, but without the tools to do so.

We have covered many of the tools already in this book – the Training 4 Influence methodology was literally developed to be one of them. The skills and knowledge to undertake the role and delivering services from a values-based perspective are both important tools, but there is a key component that I haven't mentioned yet: the importance of supporting people to have professional emotional resilience.

CASE EXAMPLE

Some years ago, I was employed as a trainee forensic psychologist, working with people in prison. At the same time, my marriage was breaking down. I had dropped three dress sizes and was stressed beyond belief, although I didn't recognise it.

As I was a trainee, I was employed on the minimum wage, so I took on additional work as an assistant manager in a bar. I would head straight from my day job to the bar, and then, more or less, straight from the bar to my day job.

At the time, I thought I was on top of everything, but I really wasn't. Fortunately for me, my day job manager recognised what was going on and made me take four weeks' leave. She also signed me up to see a counsellor through my work to help me build my emotional resilience, and helped me get some work on a Saturday doing IQ testing, so that I was able to give up my bar job.

I hadn't realised it at the time, but I was on a course for burnout with no insight as to what was happening. My manager was able to step in and use her insight to stop me from slipping. I am forever grateful to her.

It's so important when we work in such demanding roles that we develop good emotional resilience ourselves *and* to be able to look out for our colleagues. Professional emotional resilience can be defined as our capacity to thrive in situations of high demand and ongoing pressure, to bounce back from significant challenges, difficulties and setbacks, and to use them for learning and growth in the workplace.

Having professional and personal emotional resilience is vital to anyone working in criminal justice, social care and education. Apart from enabling us to develop mechanisms which protect us against overwhelming experiences, it can prevent us from becoming mentally unwell. Other benefits include improved physical health, leading to reduced sick absence, and improved learning. And, as the saying goes, 'You can't pour from an empty cup.' Without high levels of resilience, we can't give our best to the customers we work with.

The different skills necessary for developing this ability to bounce back are self-reflection and self-awareness, problem-solving, emotional intelligence, social confidence and social support. At Taye, we weave measures to increase professional resilience through all of our core sessions. When we cover emotional resilience and burnout, we find older workers often chip in with their own examples, and younger workers are appreciative of people sharing insight. Up until that point, they may well have thought they were the only ones feeling that way. And because we recognise that delegates may have experienced trauma themselves and/or be experiencing high levels of stress, overwhelm and possible burnout, we incorporate trauma-informed principles and practices in our training.

CASE EXAMPLE

I was involved in debriefing a facilitator who had two upset delegates on her course. One delegate had disclosed abuse; the other was concerned about a family member's situation. This isn't unusual, and it is a testament to Taye's fantastic facilitators that delegates feel able to seek their support.

This is the reality of delivering safeguarding training: it can be emotionally draining for the delegates, as well as the facilitator. In various sessions, we discuss in detail the categories of abuse, we discuss case examples, watch videos and look at lessons learned. Of course people are occasionally triggered. It can be confusing and upsetting. We always warn people of this at the beginning of the session and share self-care techniques, encouraging them to take a break when needed.

Delegates are people too, not just professionals. They have families, lives, experiences, just like service users. This is why it's important that training sessions cover emotional resilience and self-care. Safeguarding is about everybody, all of the time. If we don't look after the professionals, how can we expect them to support the customers?

Responders are usually designated safeguarding officers and/or managers, so they are perfectly placed to support and encourage staff to share their concerns. Often, they are the people expected to report these concerns to the local authority.

A good responder can make all the difference within an organisation. They can influence a culture of transparency, support and action. But often, when Taye's facilitators deliver safeguarding responder training, the delegates tell us they find the role lonely and overwhelming. We advise them to build a network of support for themselves and encourage a culture of open discussion. Safeguarding is everyone's responsibility, but a responder does have a vitally important role to play in it with clear responsibilities.

We've covered a lot of ground in this chapter. If some of the concepts are new to you or you haven't looked at them in this much detail before, I recognise there may be much for you to think about and possibly research further. But I can't stress enough how important it is to operate from a values-led perspective, both as a facilitator and a frontline worker. If you get this aspect of your service right, so much else will fall into place.

Shared personal and/or professional values help us build connections with others. Knowing what's important to us in life is what sustains us through difficult times. More than that, values give us a framework within which to operate so that our decisions are sound and consistent. Being values-led provides us with the greatest opportunity to bring about transformational change and make a difference to someone's life.

You can download some example slides and activities covering trauma-informed practices, unconscious bias and emotional resilience at https://training4influence. co.uk/resources/

CHAPTER TOP TIPS

When incorporating values in a session, consider:

- Exploring personal values
- Identifying how personal values and organisational values compare
- Including a session on the importance of valuing others, using worked examples
- Identifying what organisational values mean in practice in the workplace and what a values-led service looks like
- Discussing how values-based decision-making works in practice
- Discussing how to develop an action plan to deliver values-based decision making and a values-led service

When incorporating unconscious bias in a session, consider:

- Providing a safe space for people to speak openly without fear of judgement
- Delivering activities which help people to become more aware of any unconscious biases that they hold
- Challenging unconscious bias in a constructive, non-threatening and non-judgemental way
- Using relevant case examples to illustrate the importance of recognising unconscious bias in decision making

When incorporating a trauma-informed approach, focus your course on helping delegates to understand:

- What a trauma-informed environment is and why such an approach is needed
- How trauma can affect people and how to recognise the signs
- How trauma can affect people working with you
- What a trauma-informed approach will look like in practice for your service
- How to develop an action plan for becoming trauma informed in your practice

When you're dealing with individuals, you may need to make sure that they are aware that certain things can trigger them. This could include:

- Feeling they're not believed
- Feeling judged
- Having to retell their story numerous times
- Lack of voice or control
- Being labelled

To encourage people to be more resilient, include activities which:

- Focus on the positive aspects of their personal and working lives
- Build problem-solving skills
- Take positive steps to move them towards their goals
- Help them accept change as inevitable
- Help them learn from the past and the present
- Identify ways to improve their physical and mental wellbeing

And we have finished the methodology. I'd like to take a moment to reassure you that the process is very simple and straightforward. Whether you've been a training facilitator for three weeks or thirty years, you can use this book to learn the tools needed to deliver the methodology effectively and transform lives.

It can seem overwhelming and you may be worried that you'll lose sight of what your course is about in your quest to be all encompassing. However, chances are that you are already applying some or all of the methodology instinctively. Training 4 Influence gives you the framework to connect together all the elements, to enable the added influence.

I remember watching some of my team's faces draining of colour when I told them that using a trauma-informed approach was going to be part of the 'values' step. They were actually already delivering the practical aspects – it was the theoretical title that worried them. Once I explained what it meant they were much more relaxed.

I'm aware that we all have different learning styles and therefore reading material like this may not be the preferred way for everyone to learn something new. If this is the case please do listen to our Training 4 Influence podcasts which explains the method in detail and include interviews with those who have gone through the full programme. They talk about their fears, concerns and the transformation that has taken place.

Like many things, it's about breaking it down into bite-sized chunks to process the information. Take what you need from my book at this stage and contact me for any further information.

Re-read the book as many times as you need. The important thing to stress is that once you've processed the methodology, it's easy to use and will become so natural that you won't want to operate in any other way.

6
Delivering Training 4 Influence Online

It is not always easy to get a team together. As we move through the twenty-first century, we are seeing a rise in dispersed and remote teams: people working together who live in different areas or time zones and those who are increasingly busy with budgets that are stretched. Because of all this, we at Taye Training are seeing month on month an increase in bookings for online learning.

The pitfalls of e-learning

Firstly, it's really important that we are clear that online learning means different things to different people. Specifically there is a difference between pre-designed and/or recorded e-learning and live online learning.

E-learning is often used as a quick fix by employers. It's a cheap, easy way to tick some boxes and to say that training has been done. If you use e-learning as a means of training, you need to ask yourself if you can be sure that people have learned what they need to learn. And will they retain the information?

That's not to say that e-learning doesn't have its place. There are some good examples of e-learning done well and used appropriately. For example, if the e-learning has been developed by in-house trainers and is tailored to the organisation, it may well tick some of the right boxes. But, for the majority of subjects, there is no substitute for face-to-face training.

If all you need to do is share essential information that people can read and learn or short instructional sessions on, for example, how to use a piece of equipment or carry out a practical task, e-learning can be appropriate. But e-learning is most definitely not appropriate for other types of learning. In fact, its uses are limited, and when it's done badly, it doesn't engage people or consider how they learn best. There is no opportunity for discussion or clarification, for delegates to highlight that they haven't understood something, for debating with their fellow delegates, or for challenging and changing perceptions.

Most importantly, e-learning doesn't tend to change beliefs and behaviours. If someone holds a stereotypical belief, e-learning is unlikely to challenge that view.

If they've always behaved the same way in the presence of a particular type of person, they'll continue to behave that way because there is no one to show them another way. With e-learning, each delegate brings their own frame of reference to the training and can filter out those things that don't fit within their frame of reference.

Sitting with a group of peers and a facilitator will have a much bigger impact. Suddenly, delegates are hearing things that don't fit with their frame of reference and some of their beliefs may be challenged. It's powerful, transformational stuff that e-learning can never achieve – think back to the value expert facilitators bring to the room. Often in e-learning, people are simply focused on acquiring enough information to enable them to pass the test at the end. Then they may well promptly forget the information.

Another drawback with e-learning courses is that they tend to be a one-size-fits-all approach. They don't work in a sector which needs human-to-human interaction, consideration of grey areas and people to deal with situations where there is no one right answer, only different options to weigh up and assess. This of course applies to every sector to a greater or lesser extent, but it may be even more key for sectors working with vulnerable people, and delivering life-changing and lifesaving services requiring consideration of complex information, coupled with dynamic risk assessment, values-led decision making and application of a range of skills and techniques. How can anyone bring organisational values to life through e-learning in isolation?

I often speak passionately about the detrimental impact e-learning has had on the criminal justice and social care sectors. When the recession hit complex services, face-to-face training was one of the first things to go and many operational managers saw e-learning as a blessing. It cost next to nothing to purchase all the courses that quality assurers insisted on, no course took longer than a couple of hours, and teams could complete e-learning in their own homes without disrupting services.

CASE EXAMPLE

I remember working for a local authority and allocating a couple of work-from-home days to my new team members in their first weeks, so they could complete all their e-learning, read the big file of policies and sign to say they understood everything and were now capable of doing the job. Thinking back now, I can't believe I thought like that, but I was under pressure. I had a high staff turnover, I needed people trained and delivering services, and e-learning seemed to be the quick and simple solution.

I berate myself now. The courses comprised hours and hours of content in mostly information-based written format, none of which was values led. I clearly remember the safeguarding children e-learning course, written by an education-focused organisation that must have made a fortune. But a one-hour e-learning course focusing on the average child did not prepare my workers for the safeguarding concerns in the hostels and travellers' sites they worked on.

As a manager, at that point, I was happy that I'd ticked the box, completely naïve to the consequences. Twelve years later, I did some work for a national homeless charity and was astounded to realise the approach was still the same. On my induction, I had one day's face-to-face training and fifteen e-learning courses to complete. Of course, I completed them all, but what did I remember? Two things: never to use public Wi-Fi with the company's laptop, and which fire extinguisher to use in which circumstance. Both extremely useful bits of information, but not enough when the expectation was for me to lead teams of people working with some of society's most vulnerable.

In many of my social media posts about e-learning, I've gone further than just saying 'e-learning doesn't work'. I truly believe that the move to predominantly e-learning in social care, charities and criminal justice has had a lasting impact on how we deliver services as organisations.

Nothing teaches us how to work in such a complex sector better than learning among a group of people with mixed experiences, values, opinions, ages, cultures, motivations and frustrations. Each delegate then has their perspectives challenged, is introduced to new ideas, learns from others' mistakes and shares their own.

Let me give you an example.

CASE EXAMPLE

A brand-new care worker joins the sector straight from education. Twenty-one years old, she has limited experience. She learns only via e-learning, remembers elements of legislation and expectations, and gets on with the job.

Looking around her at work, she thinks everyone can do the job better than her. She can't remember how to do x, y and z and doesn't dare ask. She's sure she should know, and that the person she is working with knows she is new and is just being caring and considerate towards her for that reason. This is a recipe for a professional boundary disaster.

If the organisation were to give this young employee face-to-face training along with some of the members of the team she is joining (some with more experience) and a facilitator who was a care worker for twenty years, tailoring the information so it is applicable to her role, she would feel supported and learn in the training that we all struggle at times. No one knows everything and boundaries are easily blurred. She would then be more likely to discuss her worries with the team and recognise indicators of potential disasters.

This may seem extreme, but actually it's a really basic example. When you consider that e-learning removes the feeling of being part of a group, belonging to a team, having a shared mission and being truly valued for the work that you are undertaking, it's no surprise that so many frontline workers struggle with their own mental overloads, complex situations and imposter syndrome. Face-to-face training helps to build emotional resilience, allows you to learn from others and pitches training at the appropriate level.

We expect more and more from our frontline workers – people who are just people, but are acting as super-heroes with pressure being piled on them daily. When are we investing in them? Recognising their struggle? The least we can do is give them the tools they need and effective, relatable training, connect them as teams and value their gift to us. Ah, I'm loving how this book has gone full circle. I said something similar to this at the start.

Live online learning

You may, at this point, be wondering why we at Taye Training have applied Training 4 Influence to online learning. Initially, it was led by market need: the increasing difficulties people are experiencing getting together for face-to-face sessions while still needing the specialist training to deliver services safely. When we were first asked, we considered the facts but also didn't want to fall into the trap of providing a range of e-learning courses that didn't fit with our Training 4 Influence methodology. I was adamant that if we couldn't deliver courses online while meeting the Training 4 Influence standards, we wouldn't deliver them online at all. I wanted Taye to deliver online learning that is live and mimics many of the benefits of face-to-face learning not e-learning.

That's where I draw a distinction between e-learning, which is static and can be disengaging, and live online learning, which is interactive and engaging. When we at Taye started exploring whether we could apply our methodology to live online training, that meant delivery by an operational expert via an interactive platform instead of in a classroom. But I still wasn't sure this would be engaging enough.

The first thing we needed to do was to find a platform that would enable Taye facilitators to use virtual breakout rooms so that we could continue to vary how sessions were run. Initially, I was told that my researcher couldn't find a suitable platform that offered this facility, and I was upset and tearful that we couldn't go ahead with live online training. Even though we had customers already waiting to book, I wasn't willing to reduce our standards.

Fortunately, she rang back twenty minutes later to tell me that she had been wrong. There were online platforms that offered breakout facilities. We had the platform and our facilitators were happy to deliver for us in this way, so the next step was to adapt our courses for live online learning without compromising on content and quality.

Through the pilot process, we were still tailoring our live online learning to the organisations we were working with and to the specific roles of the delegates attending. In addition to this, we needed to make sure that the courses would continue to be interactive and engaging.

We put lots of thought into working out how to make that happen, including looking at how we could vary things by using the breakout facility to do paired and group activities, and the screen sharing facility to show slides. We wanted to inject movement into the sessions, too, as normally people are active when they attend our courses in person, and we didn't want to lose that. We now do our values and attitudes exercise by asking people to stand up or sit down in front of their screen according to whether they agree or disagree with the statement that the facilitator reads out. Another popular online activity is bingo, where we ask delegates to use household items as their counters. Everyone loves a good quiz.

All the online sessions are shorter than the face-to-face ones, with more breaks. There is usually a little preparation work for delegates to do before the session and a long lunch break with an activity involved. We have to recognise that people may be learning in their own homes, potentially with children or other household members around.

Because they are operational experts themselves, the facilitators have put a lot of effort into ensuring the courses are delivered remotely in a way that they would like to receive them if they were the delegates. We've worked through all our courses, adapting them for live online learning.

One thing that has helped us ensure online delivery runs smoothly is to treat it the same as face-to-face delivery as much as possible, particularly with regards to the preparation. We recommend the facilitator logs on up to an hour before the session starts to check everything is working, that the PowerPoint still runs smoothly and that they have links and files saved in a folder in the background for easy access to share when needed. It's no different to turning up to a venue and checking the laptop and projector work, that you have Wi-Fi password, all handouts in the right order on the table in front of you, pens and toys etc. During online delivery people often turn up early, so it's reassuring for them to be greeted by the introductory slide and some background music. Much of the process is just as it would be for face-to-face training and sometimes this provides even more space for delegates to keep themselves safe during emotive discussions and to contribute without feeling judged.

One of our facilitators recently told me that she loves online training because it is easier for her as a facilitator to include everybody in the discussions. She explained it is simple for her to see everyone's face and name on the screen while talking through the slides etc. She is aware of those that aren't as quick to raise their hands and unmute their mics to answer questions or join in with the discussions and so, for the next question or activity, she can direct it to those people specifically by asking them by name what they think or their thoughts on the matter.

CASE EXAMPLE

We recently delivered a mentoring course and, though it was for online delivery, all the aspects within the methodology were still applied. The facilitator still spoke with the client beforehand to understand what they needed from the course, how long had they been mentoring and who, and the mission and objectives of the mentoring.

It was still very much tailored to the client, and we still had those discussions/activities based on their values with time for reflection. We also managed a role play activity which the delegates were able to complete in their groups in the breakout rooms. At one point the group were watching a video which was very emotive, and a delegate sent the facilitator a private message to say it had really gotten to her. The facilitator was able to message her privately during the video to ensure she was OK and encouraged her to go make a coffee and step away from the computer for a few minutes.

Once the video had finished the delegates went into breakout rooms for an activity. While the other delegates were completing the activity, the facilitator was then able to create a room for her to go into to benefit from a chat/debrief. Alongside this, she was able to visit the other rooms to check the activity discussions. The delegate's situation was kept private as the other team members assumed she was in one of the other breakout groups.

And you too can deliver Training 4 Influence live online if you follow the techniques in this book and apply them remotely – just like we have:

- All material is delivered by an experienced facilitator who is an operational expert in the subject matter.

- Interactive and engaging sessions take account of individual learning styles and involve paired work, group work and other activities where people move about. They also use accelerated learning techniques to hold delegates' interest and maximise the opportunity for learning.

- The material is tailored so that it's applicable to the roles of the people attending, meaning that they can relate case examples and learning to what they do. Everything relates back to their roles and the policies, principles and process of the organisation.

- Values-led sessions focus on the importance of organisational values, along with the values that are important to delegates and how they value others. This makes for better, more informed decision making.

Within two weeks of a customer's request for live online training, we at Taye can now adapt any course for online delivery using the Training 4 Influence methodology. How do we do that? With a wonderful team of facilitators: people who want to make the most of every opportunity to support their colleagues and help other frontline workers to feel confident and able to deliver their services properly.

Delivering online has been an intense learning curve for our facilitators, the delegates and me, but we are all doing our best to meet the ever-changing needs of the customer group. We are all now living at least partially in an online world and teams are becoming more remote by the day. Not all Taye facilitators deliver this way. Some are still more comfortable in a face-to-face environment, but others love the flexibility of being able to deliver from home to people across the world. You can decide what works for you. I never really expected to apply the Training 4 Influence methodology to live online learning, but the course adaptations we've made work, and mean we have removed barriers so more people can access our training. And in addition to all the benefits of the Training 4 Influence methodology, live online learning helps people to connect to their colleagues when they are not working together in an office environment.

If you develop quality online learning, you'll help to build strong remote teams and make people feel more connected to their colleagues and to the organisation.

Just as importantly, people will learn and retain the information much more effectively than they would from one-size-fits-all e-learning, leading to higher-performing teams.

Maybe if Taye's customers had not made the request, we wouldn't have considered live online training, but now we're really glad that they did. It took us out of our comfort zone, so we've had to learn too. It's shown our customers that we are responsive to their needs and enables us to provide much-needed training to the sector using our Training 4 Influence methodology. And we believe that our methodology can transform live online learning, just like it can face-to-face learning. We can now let our customers decide how they want to receive their training and we'll keep focusing on feedback to make sure we're delivering what they need and identify any opportunities for improvement. Just like our delegates and you, the reader, we are learning new skills every day.

CHAPTER TOP TIPS

I'll always be a strong advocate for face-to-face learning, but live online learning can deliver that face-to-face element, even if everyone involved in the training is behind a screen. We can still see one another, talk to one another, challenge ourselves and others, ask questions, share views and opinions, laugh, grow and learn together. In other words, we remain connected to one another.

If you're looking to develop your own live online learning, please bear these points in mind:

- Learn the technology first. If you decide to use Zoom and/or Slido, you are welcome to Taye's free facilitator and delegate guides at https://training4influence.co.uk/resources/. Both have video and text explanations.

- Download our free top tips for online delivery guide at https://training4influence.co.uk/resources/

- Be prepared to invest some time into adapting your usual sessions. Death by PowerPoint didn't work in face-to-face training, and will work even less in live online training.

- Have realistic expectations. Your delegates may be engaging in the session in their own homes.

- Remove any barriers to non-engagement:

  - Send out clear, simple instructions on the technology needed.

  - Make the handouts amendable so they can be completed online and no printing is needed.

- Review your training against the Training 4 Influence standards. You may need to think creatively, but it's possible. If we at Taye can do it, you can too.

  - Make sure when you're developing live online learning that it will deliver the course objectives.

  - Make sure that the live online learning is tailored to the organisation and teams you're going to be working with.

  - Use a platform that allows for breakout sessions so that you can continue to offer different types of activity to ensure learning is interactive and engaging.

- Continue to focus on delivering sessions that are values-led, because that is paramount to learning.

- Consider whether you are the right person to develop the live online learning. Are you an operational expert in the area? Are you practised enough in the technology you are planning to use?

Conclusion

As we come to the end of this book, I want to thank you, the reader, for taking the time to invest in yourself and the way that you deliver training. The world is moving on quickly, we all seem to have less free time, and so we need to actively choose where we spend that time. I feel privileged that you've spent hours of your life reading my thoughts.

I imagine you as a passionate person, someone who likes doing their best, really wants their training to hit the mark and loves seeing lightbulb moments among the people you train. I imagine you recognising yourself for the expert you are and focusing on delivering the sessions you have the right operational experience for, bringing them alive to enable the delegates to explore techniques and feel safe in their learning.

Although the Training 4 Influence methodology will improve any training session, in any sector, on any subject, it was developed specifically to be a creative solution, a way to add influence during precious training days, in an over-challenged criminal justice and social care sector. By delivering training this way, you are supporting, valuing, teaching and inspiring delegates and truly making a difference. You are giving them everything they need to deliver exceptional, safe, values-based frontline services to some of the most complex and vulnerable people in society. That's pretty special. Thank you.

If you are interested in finding out more about the methodology please visit our website www.training4influence.co.uk where you can find information about the accredited Training 4 Influence course, assess your own training against the methodology and find links to our podcast and resources.

We also have a free Training 4 Influence community on Facebook, I hope to see you there.

Acknowledgements

To every person feeling powerless in their lives, accessing services and wondering if things will change: you are not less. Keep going, have faith – things can get better.

To every professional working on the frontline, you're doing an amazing job, thank you.

To all facilitators and trainers reading this book – together we can make a difference.

Thank you to:

Faye, the yin to my yang – I couldn't have done any of this without you and I'm truly grateful to have you as my business partner and best friend.

My husband Tim, and daughters Charla and Katelyn, for the never ending patience and love you show me.

Jane – thank you for starting the domino effect that enabled me to transform my life. Connection. Opportunity. Environment. Who knew that that one decision you made in 1996 would lead to a book!

The Taye Team – without your experience, values, passion and true commitment to delivering training that really influences, this method and its impact would never have been realised.

And finally Gillian, for helping me find these words.

The Author

Tammy Banks' personal history, academic achievements and work experience have driven her to champion the importance of effective, achievable solutions to prevent abuse and poverty. Tammy leads with passion and commitment, recognising the importance of advocating for change while delivering operational solutions.

Tammy is co-director of Taye Training and developed the methodology Training 4 Influence. She is also a lay member on the Parliamentary Committee for Standards and Interim Consultant Director for the Association of Child Protection Professionals. Her TEDx talk 'Why Kindness Makes All The Difference' can be found on YouTube at bit.ly/ WhyKindnessMakesALLtheDifference

Tammy lives in Yorkshire with her two daughters and husband Tim.

Connect with Tammy and Taye Training at:

🌐 www.tayetraining.org.uk

in Tammy Banks

f Tammy Banks

🐦 Tammy Banksy

Printed in Great Britain
by Amazon